MOVING
YOUR CHURCH

Become a Spirit-Led Community

Also by S. Joseph Kidder

Majesty: Experiencing Authentic Worship

The Big Four: Secrets to a Thriving Church Family

Youth Speaks: The Church Listens

MOVING YOUR CHURCH

Become a Spirit-Led Community

S. JOSEPH KIDDER

Pacific Press®
Publishing Association

Nampa, Idaho | Oshawa, Ontario, Canada
www.pacificpress.com

Cover design resources from iStockphoto.com
Inside design by Aaron Troia

The author assumes full responsibility for the accuracy of all facts and quotations as cited in this book.

You can obtain additional copies of this book by calling toll-free 1-800-765-6955 or by visiting http://www.adventistbookcenter.com.

Library of Congress Cataloging-in-Publication Data:
Kidder, S. Joseph, 1953-
  Moving your church : become a spirit-led community / S. Joseph Kidder.
     pages cm
  ISBN 978-0-8163-5785-7 (pbk.)
1. Church growth. 2. Pastoral theology. I. Title.
  BV652.25.K53 2015
  253—dc23
                                        2015030986

October 2015

Dedication

To my wife, Denise, and my children, Jason and Stephanie,
the joy of my life.

Acknowledgment

I am so grateful to my able research assistant, Kristy Hodson,
who read the whole manuscript and gave valuable insights to improve it.
Kristy, you have been a blessing to me and my work.

Contents

Introduction
Does Your Church Have a Purpose?

"You are a chosen people, a royal priesthood, a holy nation, God's special possession, that you may declare the praises of him who called you out of darkness into his wonderful light. Once you were not a people, but now you are the people of God; once you had not received mercy, but now you have received mercy."—1 Peter 2:9, 10

"The church is God's appointed agency for the salvation of men. It was organized for service, and its mission is to carry the gospel to the world. From the beginning it has been God's plan that through His church shall be reflected to the world His fullness and His sufficiency. The members of the church, those whom He has called out of darkness into His marvelous light, are to show forth His glory. The church is the repository of the riches of the grace of Christ; and through the church will eventually be made manifest, even to 'the principalities and powers in heavenly places,' the final and full display of the love of God. Ephesians 3:10."—Ellen White[1]

At a lay leadership training seminar I was conducting, someone asked, "What is the purpose of the church?" I inquired of the audience what they thought. They gave various answers: "The church exists to proclaim the messages of the three angels," "to preach the truth," "to meet the needs of my family and me," "to build community," and "to spread the gospel and teach about Jesus."

As I reflected on this question, I recalled that Jesus said He came to earth "to seek and to save the lost" (Luke 19:10, RSV). Matthew tells us that just before Jesus left, He revealed the part we are to play in His mission. "Go and make disciples of all nations," He said, "baptizing them in the name of the Father and of the Son and of the Holy Spirit, and teaching them to obey everything I have commanded you" (Matthew 28:19, 20). I'm convinced that this is the purpose of the church. Those who claim to be His disciples today are here to carry on Jesus' mission of seeking and saving the lost.

We fulfill this mission best through four activities: evangelizing, worshiping, preaching, and planting churches. Most churches do some of these things, but many of them spend little time thinking about why they're doing them and how they can do them most productively. It's the responsibility of the leaders of the church to edify, equip, and train church members to carry out these tasks.

Every segment of society should be pulsating with Christian life—full of groups of committed Christians loving, serving, praying, growing, and reaching out together. When the church is functioning well, it embodies the hope of the world moved by a loving and accepting spirit. When local churches focus on fulfilling the Great Commission, they become sources of new life.

The message of the Bible is addressed to all humankind. God's revelation in Christ is still relevant today. The Holy Spirit illumines the minds of people in every place and culture. He calls us out of darkness and into light (1 Peter 2:9). He anoints and empowers believers and softens the hearts of those being reached with the gospel. God commissions every believer to work with the Holy Spirit for the purpose of showing His saving love and forgiveness to all of His children.

The chapters you are about to read are appropriate for everyone in your church—pastors, leaders, and members. They're appropriate for you because God has a place for you in your church—a task for you to do. This book will thrill your heart with inspiring stories and practical, proven methods of evangelism that work. It will challenge you to get involved in some form of ministry so you can make a difference in your community. Through the power of the Spirit, ordinary people like you and me can do extraordinary things for God.

----

1. Ellen G. White, *The Acts of the Apostles* (Mountain View, Calif.: Pacific Press®, 1911), 9.

Section One
Effective and Efficient Leadership

Every church needs the backbone that strong leaders provide. (When I speak of leaders, I have in mind not only pastors but also the officers of the church and any other of its members who have the ability to gather a group of people and direct their activities.) To be effective, these leaders must always be looking for ways in which to enhance the abilities that God has given them. To show others God's love and to be able to speak about its saving power, they must be able to connect with God and their community. For example, elders are to demonstrate a ministry of presence in the home and in hospitals. And Sabbath School leaders are often influential in sparking discussions and critical thinking among the members.

Chapter one focuses on five qualities possessed by leaders that help a church become effective and healthy: passion for a continual connection with God, ability to communicate the gospel, skill to cast a vision successfully, competency at bringing about change, and both charisma and ability that enable them to lead and influence others.

Chapter two deals with ways in which leaders build healthy relationships with their fellow church members. Special attention is given to loving their people, expressing that love, and praying and caring for those within the leader's circle of influence.

Chapter 1
The Five Essential Qualities of
Highly Effective Leaders

"David shepherded them with integrity of heart; with skillful hands he led them."—Psalm 78:72

There are many excellent books on the subjects of leadership, administration, and management. My intent here is to consider five essential qualities of effective leaders and pastors. These characteristics were gleaned from interviews with ninety-two pastors. Twenty-three of them had healthy, growing churches,[1] and sixty-nine had churches that were plateauing or declining.

An effective pastor—paid or volunteer—is someone who is led by the Spirit, anointed by God, and successful in leading his or her church to health and growth through a compelling vision and the equipping of the laity to do great things for God. We have been able to pinpoint some of the traits common to pastors who lead growing and healthy churches. While each quality is important, it is their collective strength that made the difference in leadership.

1. Effective pastors have a passion for a continual connection with God

Our interviews showed that effective pastoral leadership rests on the foundation of a personal relationship with Jesus Christ that is maintained daily. These pastors continue to develop an intense and meaningful intimacy with Jesus. One said, "It is my desire to get my heart warmed by the sweet fires of the Spirit before I engage in the rest of the activities of the day." Another insisted, "I need to feel the heavy presence of God in my life so I can influence others for Jesus."

When the effective pastors were asked how much time they spend with God each day, they said they invest about one hour praying, reading Scripture, singing, and worshiping God. In addition, many of them devote another hour to praying for their churches, members, communities, and families. These pastors pursue other spiritual disciplines (regular fasting, spiritual retreats, journaling, family worship, etc.) and are involved with others in accountability groups (prayer partners, small groups, etc.). They are earnestly seeking to grow in their relationship with Christ and to inspire their congregations to do the same. They felt that they couldn't lead people to the well of life if they hadn't drunk from it themselves recently.

Conversely, we found that pastors of declining churches spend less than half an hour with God each day. They felt that their work responsibilities made it necessary to limit their time with God. They said that pastoring requires hard work and good management.

Church members are less likely to challenge a pastor who possesses the appropriate skills and a wealth of experience. However, while skill and experience are both important and shouldn't be minimized, being Spirit-filled and Spirit-led proved to be more significant to effective pastoral leadership. Successful pastors were spiritually authentic; they recognized that their power doesn't come from their personality or giftedness; it comes from God, who called them.

Growing churches are very strong spiritually. We saw this spirituality in the leadership, organization, and driving power of the pastor who followed the biblical principle of demonstrating true spiritual concern for others. "Keep watch over yourselves and all the flock of which the Holy Spirit has made you overseers. Be shepherds of the church of God, which he bought with his own blood" (Acts 20:28). Leaders can't keep watch over others until they have looked after themselves. A pastor can lead other people in spiritual things only in proportion to his or her own understanding and experience.

2. Effective pastors can communicate the gospel successfully

Members and seekers first recognize a pastor's capacity for communication through his or her preaching. We saw that effective pastors spent a minimum of fifteen hours weekly in sermon preparation, while the less effective pastors spent about five hours each week on their sermons. Important as was the time spent in sermon preparation, other factors were just as important for good preaching. These included being aware of the needs and issues that their listeners were struggling with, being able to touch the heart, and knowing how to bring fresh insights from the Bible. The interviews suggested that inspiring preaching produces a vibrant atmosphere that excites people, drawing them to attend church themselves and to bring friends with them. I heard the following statements from members of growing churches:

- "I love my pastor. He makes the Bible come alive."
- "He's interesting to listen to, yet he is very deep."
- "He spent a lot of time in prayer, study, and preparation."

- "He leads me to a better relationship with God."
- "I am fed spiritually."
- "I feel the need for change when I am in the worship service."

For some pastors, communicating well comes naturally, but everyone can improve their skills by cultivating them. Pastors of thriving churches read for at least one hour each day, and they practice their sermons two or three times before preaching them in worship services. They also met with creative people who helped them craft better sermons and explore various ways to share the gospel. Both members and effective pastors agreed that thirty minutes or thereabout was the optimal length for sermons that drew people back.

When we asked pastors what qualities in sermons connected with people, they said the following:

- Sermons that teach us something new. Sermons that bring new insights from the biblical text or the working of God in the world today.
- Sermons that thrill the heart with the gospel and with hope.
- Sermons that awe the listeners with the greatness and majesty of God.
- Sermons that inspire the audience to do something for God and for other people.
- Sermons that connect people with God and help them to live a holy life and serve God in the world.

Church members also said they'd like to tell their pastors:

- Preach from your personal journey so your messages are genuine. Always reflect upon how the text and God have affected your life.
- Be a model of a deeply spiritual person.
- Pray more.
- Recognize the power of your works—what you do.
- Give 100 percent of your effort.
- Don't neglect your family.
- Check your motives.
- Do your research.
- Make the message clear, simple, and interesting, focusing on just one suggested action and one benefit.
- Show your sense of humor, but don't try so hard to be funny that you get too cutesy.
- Talk on a level everyone can understand.
- Don't ever quit—you *do* make a difference.

Finally, here are five rules that we gathered from interviewing and listening to good communicators:

Rule 1. Preach with passion and conviction. Believe to the depth of your being what you are preaching.

Rule 2. Preach to two people: one who is hearing what you're saying for the first time, and one who is hearing it for the last time. Preaching to the first one will make you seeker-friendly so you'll use terms and language that non-Christians and nominal Christians can understand and relate to. And preaching to the second will fill your sermon with urgency.

Rule 3. Preach biblical sermons that are relevant. Some preachers' sermons are biblical but not relevant to life today. The combination of the two is the essence of effective preaching.

Rule 4. Preach simple yet challenging sermons. Make the sermon so simple that everyone can understand it and yet challenging enough that it motivates people to action.

Rule 5. Think from the point of view of the listener. A pastor well known for his speaking ability told me that he thinks, not like a theologian, but from the point of view of a gas-station attendant who came to church out of curiosity or the wife who comes to church without her husband or the man who is tempted to compromise at work. An effective pastor said, "I always think of their need and the words of hope and comfort I give to them from the Lord."

3. Effective pastors can cast the vision successfully

Pastors aren't just preaching to inform but are also consistently communicating the vision to the church in a simple, holistic, and captivating way. One pastor said that a person who has a compelling vision "believes that our best days are ahead and that God can perform remarkable acts in our midst." Every effective pastor that we interviewed had a clear vision for his or her church and knew exactly how to take that church from where it was to where God wanted it to be. They readily led the church in this process, but they recognized it was the responsibility of the entire body of Christ to bring it to fruition.

I noticed that in many of the growing churches, the vision was cast every Sabbath with interesting stories, biblical metaphors, slogans, banners, songs, skits, and so forth. One pastor labeled it "creative redundancy." It became very clear to me that everyone knew the vision and was thrilled not only to buy in to it but also to live it.

When we interviewed members about the vision of their church, they articulated the vision and then affirmed, "We have a great vision at our church, and everyone knows what it is." At one growing congregation, I asked a ten-year-old girl if she could tell me their vision. She immediately responded, "Our church's vision is to save the world." There is no church growth without compelling vision.

Here are some vision statements I found in Seventh-day Adventist churches that are growing:

"Love God, love others, and serve the world."

"To be passionate about God's love for the lost and to become active in His ministry locally and globally."

"To connect people with the Father."

"To see every person become actively involved in ministry and witnessing."

"Sharing the Christ who cares, together."

"To pursue the lost with a passion, and to love one another because God loves us."

On the other hand, very few of the pastors, leaders, and members of plateauing or declining churches knew the mission or the vision of their church. In one interview, I called the head elder and asked him whether he knew the vision of his church. His response was, "No, but if you are interested I can get it for you."

I said, "Well, just tell me the main ideas."

"I can't do it off the top of my head," he confessed.

The vision doesn't have to be perfect, but it needs to be clear. We noted three elements of effective vision casting. First, the leader was confident about the vision, believing it to be true based upon his or her sense of God's vision. This confidence was based on prayer, Bible study, and deep reflection on the condition and history of the church and its community. Second, the vision was communicated with passion and inspiration. Third, it was simple and memorable.

Effective pastors successfully communicate the gospel and the vision of the church in inspiring ways.

4. Effective pastors can bring about change

Leaders with this competency create an environment conducive of change, lead the process successfully, and anchor the change in the congregation's culture. We discovered that many of the growing churches we studied had been sick, some so diseased that they were dying, but God used a leader and circumstances to revive them.

Leaders open to change practice critical thinking. They aren't mere reflectors of other people's ideas, plans, programs, and visions. Too many pastors, because of their lack of time or skills, are doing little critical thinking and reflection. In their effort to grow their churches, they copy existing models and expend their energies on promoting programs. The mission of the churches these people lead becomes conducting programs rather than saving souls. Assessing the situation, asking critical and thoughtful questions, and coming up with solutions to meet the urgent needs of our time are at the heart of leadership. Spiritual leaders ask three basic questions:

- Where is God working? (They want to know so they can join Him there.)
- How can we be more effective in what we do?
- What are we doing that isn't effective anymore?

Pastors need to have the courage to end activities that are no longer effective or to repurpose an activity so it can be effective again. Critical thinking will help them move their churches from stagnation to creativity and innovation.

One pastor noted, "There is no church growth without meaningful change." In an age when mission consciousness is lost in the church, it is essential for the pastor to be able to lead the congregation to become a "mission outpost." Our interviews revealed that pastors of growing churches helped their members reclaim their role in bringing people to faith in Christ. They highlighted a God-given cause that galvanized the congregation and kept unity through change. Their model didn't feature the pastor as the sole evangelist. Instead, his role was to exemplify evangelism to the members and to equip them as evangelists.

Changing a church is very difficult. It brings pain, criticism, and challenges. But leaders who persevere to the end reap amazing results.

5. Effective pastors have the ability to lead and influence others

Effective pastors can lead and influence other people because they have a passion for God and for people, and they talk about it with excitement and enthusiasm. In our interviews with pastors of thriving churches, it didn't take more than five minutes to feel their passion about God, people, and evangelism, and to get excited about it. Dynamic leaders have strong convictions about what they are doing, but leadership goes beyond merely having convictions to the ability to inspire others with those convictions.

Effective pastors are able to lead and influence others in the following ways: they can identify, develop, and support lay leaders. The early church was a movement led primarily by the laity. Today's pastors who are following this model rely heavily upon the ministry implied by the "priesthood of all believers." One pastor commented, "We need to learn to delegate. We need to pray that the Lord of the harvest will bring people to us who can help us in this and other responsibilities. It is impossible for us to do it alone." (See Matthew 9:35–38.) Not only will the laity help to reach the lost, but they themselves will reap the benefits of a closer walk with God and a renewed love for His children.

Interestingly, our survey showed that pastors of growing churches worked about forty-five hours per week, while those in plateauing and declining churches worked fifty to sixty hours per week.[2] Effective pastors spent their forty-five hours with intentionality, capitalizing on every opportunity to mobilize others into action for Jesus.

The survey we conducted revealed that growing churches had more than 50 percent of their members involved in meaningful ministry[3] and about 10 percent in evangelism.[4] Pastors coached members and leaders to develop and put to work their own leadership gifts. In contrast, plateauing and declining churches had only 30 percent of their members involved in ministry and less than 3 percent in evangelism.

Member involvement was increased by the leaders' intentionality in training and equipping the lay members. The survey highlighted the fact that pastors of growing churches spent up to one-third of their time equipping the laity to do ministry and evangelism—approximately ten to fifteen hours every week. In contrast, pastors of plateauing and declining churches spend fewer than two hours a week in training.

The priority of developing lay leaders was reflected in contributions of both time and money. Healthy churches devoted up to 10 percent of their budget on training and seminars. They spent this money in a variety of ways: buying DVDs and books, sending people to seminars, and bringing experts to conduct training. Many plateauing and declining churches reported that they had little or no budget for training.

Second, effective pastors lead by example. They don't just cast the vision; they embody it. One pastor told me, "I never ask my members to do anything that I'm not doing. Our strengths are used to show others what to do. Our weaknesses are used to show others how to rely on God."

Churches are inspired by pastors who lead by example. Many pastors of growing churches shared with us stories of winning their friends and neighbors to Christ. We weren't surprised, then, when we found that their members were actively involved in personal evangelism too.

Many pastors told us that the effect of their example was multiplied when they went above and beyond the call of duty. For example, when a pastor followed up on an *It Is Written* interest, his members were less inspired than when he shared a testimony about his neighbor attending the small group meetings he held at his house.

Several members we interviewed told us that they were inspired by their pastor's examples of spending time with God, of providing leadership in his home, of balanced living, of time management, and of other areas related to personal and church development.

Third, leaders take risks. They weigh the consequences of their decisions and aren't afraid of failure. Effective pastors often see opportunities that others missed. They view past "failures" as occasions to improve for their next attempt.

One pastor shared that when people told him that public evangelism didn't work anymore, he decided to do it more frequently than he had before. However, he modified his approach, shortening each series and making extensive use of lay leadership. His church experienced tremendous growth because of the risk they took.

Effective pastors are also decisive leaders. They're willing to take a stand on important but controversial issues. One pastor said to me, "When it comes to difficult decisions, don't be afraid of expressing your ideas and feelings. Always take a stand. But then always connect, even with those who disagree with you. Relationships always trump everything else. Finally, do not be anxious or lose sleep over it. It is not about you, but about the kingdom of God. He is in charge of His church, and He will take care of it."

Leadership is a much bigger thing than merely holding a position or having a title. The pastor is a leader by virtue of what he does rather than what position he holds. Pastors are called to know how to work with and through people, how to minister to people, and how to lead people. Our research revealed that highly effective pastors have five essential leadership qualities: the passion to continually have a connection with God, the ability to communicate the gospel, the skill to cast the vision successfully, the competency to bring about change, and the ability to lead and influence others.

While some pastors and members may naturally possess some of the leadership qualities mentioned in this chapter, all can develop and improve their leadership abilities with intentionality and the guidance of the Holy Spirit. If leaders want to grow others, they must be growing themselves.

---

1. Our definition of growth is a 3 percent increase in membership, baptisms, and attendance for a minimum of three years.

2. These statistics didn't include ministry done during Sabbath hours.

3. Our survey defined *ministry* as consistent involvement and planning in church programs and functions, and leadership such as teaching in Sabbath School, organizing special events, involving themselves in community services and church choir, and so forth.

4. Our survey defined *evangelism* as consistent involvement in witnessing through activities such as giving Bible studies, sharing their testimony with others, distributing literature, conducting or assisting with evangelistic meetings in the local church, and leading or assisting with the visitor and new-believer Sabbath School class.

Chapter 2
It's All About Relationships

"Keep watch over yourselves and all the flock of which the Holy Spirit has made you overseers. Be shepherds of the church of God, which he bought with his own blood."—Acts 20:28

"May the Lord make your love increase and overflow for each other and for everyone else, just as ours does for you."—1 Thessalonians 3:12

The relationship that pastors have with their people is one of the most sacred that there is. God is honored when His people are satisfied with their pastor and when the pastor has a positive attitude toward them. God wants pastors and their members to love each other, to pray for each other, to work together, to serve together, to worship together, and to win souls together. Below are some suggestions that may be of help to pastors who are working to develop a healthy relationship with their people.

1. Love your people

I interviewed a pastor who had more than forty years' worth of successful pastoral experience. I asked him to tell me two things he had learned during his career. He said, "I can sum up pastoral work in two lines: love God with all your heart, mind, and soul; and love others as you love yourself. To be a successful pastor, one must love God and love people."

Paul had this kind of affection toward his people. He remembered them fondly. He prayed for them. And he built strong partnerships with them so they could spread the gospel (Philippians 1:3–5). When you don't love the people God has entrusted to you, they will feel it and see through any facade you may be trying to erect. Ask God to give you a heart full of love for the people you serve.

2. Express your love for your people

As a pastor, I told my congregations repeatedly—from the pulpit and from other venues—that I loved them and prayed for them continually. Whether your church has thirty-five members or a thousand, every one of them needs to know that you value them.

When I was a pastor, I spent two to three hours every week writing notes of encouragement to the people in my churches. I wrote notes to people on their anniversaries and their birthdays and when they volunteered to do something that improved our community or our church.

In one of the churches I pastored, there was a woman who was married to a seeker who came to church occasionally. This woman led out in the church's Vacation Bible School, and when it concluded, to show our love and appreciation, the church sent both of them to an all-expense-paid retreat. The seeker was so touched that when they returned from their little vacation, he asked to study the Bible with me. Several months later I had the privilege of baptizing him. Expressing appreciation is a form of blessing that touches both parties.

3. Pray for your people

The pastor should pray for each of his people, especially those who have burdens and heartaches. When a couple is having trouble, the pastor should pray for them. When Johnny has the measles or Mary has the mumps, the pastor should call on them and pray for them. Many times a little note of encouragement or a phone call proves to be a great blessing.

When I was a pastor, I spent Mondays praying for my church and community. I lifted up each member by name, called them to tell them I was praying for them, and asked whether there was anything they wanted me to pray about. Praying for church members in this way kills conflict and brings forgiveness and love to the church.

4. Build your people, not yourself

Some pastors think of the church they're currently serving as a stepping-stone to a bigger and more prominent ministry. Don't use your people to build a great ministry; use your ministry to build great people. The greatest product of a pastor's ministry is a steadfast Christian who grows in the grace of the Lord. Individuals are important. They matter infinitely to God, so they must matter to us too. When preachers love their people and rejoice more over their growth than over anything else, it is apparent that they have developed the heart of a true pastor.

5. Care for your people

Remember that people are more important than programs, money, or the church building and facilities. People like to feel that they are loved and cared for.

Some pastors say they're into programming, techniques, and strategies. All of these are important, but they're not what makes a church productive. When you have a church that is filled with great people who love Jesus and reflect His grace, you have a church that is filled with blessings and that is growing naturally. Spend time with your members, fellowship with them, love them, pray for them, and seek their good. Do less programming and more discipling. If you do, your members will grow and the church will prosper.

When I arrived at one of the churches I pastored, it had an attendance of about forty and a debt of about $100,000, and it was full of conflict. But I showed love and care for the congregation, I fed them spiritually, I prayed for them continually, and I gave them opportunities to grow.

I pastored that church for twelve years. When I left, we had an attendance of about five hundred, we had no debt—in fact, we had about sixty thousand dollars in the bank, and we had an environment full of harmony and joy. At the farewell party the church members put on for us, they didn't mention any of that stuff. Instead, one after another, they came to us and said, "Thank you for loving us, for being with us, and for making church a fun place to be."

Section Two
Growing the Family

Section two begins with an investigation of what forms of church growth work in Seventh-day Adventist churches today. I discovered that the churches that are growing are combining traditional methods of evangelism with some more innovative ideas that resonate with their communities.

The second chapter in this section discusses what constitutes a culture of evangelism. The point is that evangelism isn't something that is restricted to professionals who specialize in preaching and in conducting complicated campaigns. Rather, in churches in which the genuine culture of evangelism flourishes, bringing people to Jesus has become the way of life for every member. This chapter explores the fuel, atmosphere, power, blueprint, heart, glue, model, and inspiration needed to foster a culture of evangelism.

Next, we look back at what worked for Jesus and discover that His methods of evangelism still work today. He met people where they were rather than expecting them to search Him out. He focused on getting to know them as individuals and meeting their needs.

In the chapter titled "Friendship Evangelism," you'll read the story of how God used a poodle to bring a family into relationship with Him. Evangelism doesn't have to be complicated.

And the final chapter of this section shows that evangelism is being done through the creating of relationships and by turning the workplace into a place of witnessing.

Chapter 3
Insights From Fast-Growing Churches

"The sons of Issachar [were] men who understood the times with knowledge of what Israel should do."—1 Chronicles 12:32, NASB

For many church members, the word *evangelism* refers to meetings held in the church for a few weeks of every year or two. Churches pour a lot of time, energy, and resources into these efforts—sometimes with good results, but often with little to show for their efforts. Whatever the case, many church members view evangelism as a church program rather than a way of life. Many churches lack the comprehensive strategy necessary to reach their community. Consequently, like the Evangelicals, 80 percent of the Seventh-day Adventist churches in North America are plateauing or declining.[1] This means that the Adventist Church isn't growing fast enough to keep up with the growth of the general population.[2]

The purpose of this chapter is to outline some of the challenges we face in the North American Division today and then to develop a model for evangelistic ministry that can overcome these challenges. This model will be based primarily on research I have conducted on growing churches in the NAD,[3] on what I experienced while pastoring growing churches,[4] on teaching seminary classes on church growth, and on my study of this topic. By the word *evangelism* I mean an attempt to win others for the kingdom of God by leading them to believe in Jesus Christ and to follow Him as His disciples (Matthew 28:19). Even though the research presented here describes churches in North America, the principles regarding effective evangelism are universal and can be applied to any church in any town or village around the world.

The challenges we face

1. Public evangelism is not as effective as it used to be. Monte Sahlin, who researches trends in the North American Division, told me the results of some studies he's been working on recently. He said that while the percentage of churches reporting involvement in public evangelism has increased, the number of baptisms per evangelistic meeting has decreased.[5] One reason may be the fact that the number of people who, without previous relational contact, are willing to attend evangelistic meetings and then join the church is decreasing.[6]

Traditionally, the church has relied on the mailing of handbills to generate attendance at evangelistic meetings, but handbills are becoming less effective. Several studies have suggested that the ratio of response to handbills distributed through the mail is a thousand to one. In other words, to draw ten nonmembers to an evangelistic meeting, one must mail ten thousand handbills.[7] In fact, in many places today, those numbers may be considered generous. In my analysis of seven recent evangelistic series, I found that the ratio of response was one respondent per two thousand handbills.

2. Most Adventists aren't engaged in relational evangelism. Studies of the witnessing of Evangelicals by Thom Rainer revealed that only 2 percent of the members invite an unchurched person to church in a given year. That means 98 percent of church-goers never extend an invitation to a seeker throughout the year. Seven out of ten unchurched people have never been invited to attend a church.[8] The 235 interviews my team and I did led us to conclude that these statistics fit the Adventist context too. Our interviews uncovered some of the reasons church members didn't witness to other people: lack of spirituality, busyness, fear of rejection, and lack of know-how.

3. Most churches don't have a comprehensive evangelistic strategy. In our study of a sample of ninety-two Seventh-day Adventist churches in North America, we found that 75 percent of them didn't have a comprehensive evangelistic strategy. In effect, the churches existed to serve their members only. Church was a one-time event each week, and the members made little or no attempt to draw the community to the church.

Our survey asked, "If we took your church out of your community, would they miss you?" Sixty-nine of the churches—75 percent of them—said, "They don't even know we're here."

An effective model for evangelism

1. Focus on discipleship for effective evangelism. All growing Seventh-day Adventist churches that we studied in North America focus on discipleship. They recognize disciple-making as New Testament evangelism. Jesus described the core of discipleship in these words: " 'Love the Lord your God with all your heart and with all your soul and with all your mind.' This is the first and greatest commandment. And the second is like it: 'Love your neighbor as yourself' " (Matthew 22:37–39).

Christian discipleship is the process by which followers of Jesus grow in knowledge of Him and in His grace. The Holy Spirit equips them to overcome the pressures and trials of this present life and to become more and more like Jesus—developing His love, vision, mission, and character. This process requires believers to respond to the Holy Spirit's prompting to examine their thoughts, words, and actions and to compare them with the Word of God. They grow in discipleship through developing love and commitment to Jesus and strengthening that love and commitment through spiritual disciplines such as prayer, worship, Bible reading, fellowship, ministry, and evangelism. And those who become genuine disciples share their faith. So, focusing on discipleship influences believers to be open to their transformation by the Holy Spirit, and it awakens the desire to make other disciples and supplies the means to make it happen.

A young Adventist couple who had three kids of their own felt a burden for discipling the neighborhood children. Every week they invited the neighborhood kids over for food and games and Bible stories. Usually, between eight and fifteen children attended these gatherings. Sometimes they played in their pool; and sometimes they went to the park. The couple also offered to bring the kids who were interested to church with them, and they often had to take two cars to accommodate all the children.

Maggie was one of those neighborhood kids. The Christianity she saw in that family was filled with joy and excitement. When they moved, no one came to take Maggie to church anymore, so she stopped going.

Thirty years later, Maggie, who by that time had also moved out of the old neighborhood and now had a family of her own, got a brochure in the mail about an evangelistic series I was hosting in my church. She recognized the name *Seventh-day Adventist* and came to the meetings because of her fond memories of her neighbors and of the church she had visited as a child.

Maggie loved what she was learning in those meetings, and she appreciated the acceptance she felt in the church. But she said she wasn't ready to be baptized yet, so I told her I understood and encouraged her to continue attending the services in the church and to become a greeter during those meetings.

At the close of the series, I announced that five people would be baptized the following week. Much to my surprise, Maggie showed up and said she wanted to be baptized too. When I asked why she declined before, she said that she was sharing all that she learned with her husband and had wanted to wait to be baptized with him. She said she had now reconsidered and decided to be baptized as a witness to him.

Maggie was able to track down the couple who had taken her to church. She wrote a letter to them, which she shared with our church, thanking them for their care and commitment when she was younger. She said it was because of them that she had found Christ.

Maggie's former neighbors were glad to hear from her, and they shared in her excitement. Within a few months, because of Maggie's commitment to share with and disciple her family, her husband and children also decided that they wanted to be baptized. Then Maggie felt impressed to start intentionally discipling the children in her neighborhood in much the same way as her neighbors had when she was a child. And throughout the years that followed, many of these children and their families made decisions for Christ and were baptized.

This is the essence of discipleship. As the Holy Spirit transforms believers, He works through them to transform others in their circle of influence. Focusing on discipleship takes intentionality, time, and effort, but it brings great rewards by building up healthy followers of Jesus who reproduce and thus expand the kingdom of God.

2. Emphasize relational evangelism. Evangelism isn't a program; it's a way of life. The greatest evangelistic asset for any church is members who love Jesus and are excited about their church. Relational evangelism means believers witnessing for Christ in everyday life by getting their friends and relatives into Bible studies, church fellowship groups, sports teams, and service projects. Relational evangelism is effective because it is natural and it is biblical.

In order to appeal to postmodern, secular people, evangelism must bring a message of peace, hope, and harmony. People today are so assaulted by advertisements and political messages that for them to consider something to be important and true, it must come to them in a personal, loving, and practical way. Research by Thom Rainer revealed that 82 percent of the unchurched are at least somewhat likely to attend church if they're invited by a trusted friend or family member.[9] The research I've done recently in Adventist churches in North America reveals that not only will the unchurched attend in response to relational evangelism but that relational evangelism also will eventually draw them into joining the church. The results confirmed that 70 to 80 percent of people who became members were first brought into the church through a friend or relative.[10]

In the past few decades many have realized the need for a shift to a more active personal witness. In his book *Evangelism as a Lifestyle,* Jim Peterson suggests that a simple verbalizing of the gospel message is not enough to reach secularized Americans. He says we must employ "affirmation evangelism in practice." By this he means that evangelism is "a process of modeling and explaining the Christian message. God's people must incarnate His character through their compassion and love. Then they go on to verbalize the nature of His eternal reign." Lifestyle evangelism wins people because it starts by "winning a hearing."[11]

This was evident in the research we did on the Adventist churches that are growing. They tell their members that when they become followers of Christ, they are signing up for His mission in everything they do. They are to win a hearing by doing good, caring for the poor, inviting neighbors over, building relationships with coworkers, and investing in friendships with those outside the church. Then they are to tell them the story of the gospel and what God has done in their lives. The church's role is to help Christians live such attractive lives that other people will want what they have.

James, an engineer who attended one of the churches I pastored, exemplified relational evangelism. He worked for a very large corporation, supervising more than a hundred people, yet he was also very active in the church and the community. He loved and served God passionately, preaching often, doing Bible studies, and going on mission trips.

People noticed how James's commitment to Christ touched every area of his life, and they often said, "James, you should be a pastor." James always answered, "I *am* a pastor—the only difference is that I'm paid by my company instead of by the church. No professional pastor is allowed in my engineering firm, but I'm here every day. When my employees are hurting, I hurt with them. When they are rejoicing, I rejoice with them. I pray for them on a regular basis, and I invite them over to my home. I'm a disciple of Jesus Christ disguised as an engineer."

Through his ministry, James saw twenty of his fellow engineers come to the Lord and join the church. Relational evangelism is about disciples of Jesus Christ living out His ideals in the world disguised as nurses, teachers, cashiers, farmers, and so on. When they've built trust among those around them, they find opportunities to minister to them and to tell them what He's done for them.

3. Use multiple ways of reaching people. All twenty-three of the North American Adventist churches that are growing use multiple ways to reach people.[12] They blend relational and public evangelism with various ministries and church programs to maximize their opportunities to witness. They recognize that to reach its full potential, each form of evangelism must also use other forms. They implement a comprehensive evangelistic strategy that touches every aspect of the church's life, including Sabbath School, worship services, seasonal programs (Christmas, Easter, Mother's/Father's Day, etc.), sporting events, and all of the other ministries of the church. Each event and activity is done with the purpose of connecting people with God.

Evangelism takes place anytime, anywhere, by anyone, under any circumstances. In the doctoral classes I teach on innovative evangelism, I assign the students to see how many forms of evangelism they can find mentioned in the book of Acts. Every class has found at least fifty forms of evangelism and ministry (e.g., public evangelism to crowds, one-on-one evangelism, healing, meeting needs, and so forth). It's clear that the members of the early church lived and breathed their faith. Their passion was to win the world for Jesus. Nothing could stop them. Their evangelism was the outflow of their daily living.

Using a variety of evangelistic methods gives several benefits:

- It provides members with something to which they can invite friends and family. Our observations showed that members were much more likely to invite friends and family to a special program than to a routine service.
- It gives believers an opportunity to witness naturally. When believers invite their friends to spiritual events, they're able to talk about it afterwards.
- It reaches a broad group of seekers. Prophecy seminars appeal to some people, while Creation seminars interest others. Cooking classes reach one group effectively, while sporting events connect better with another.

A pastor who ministers in one of the growing Adventist churches that we surveyed told us that every year he and his leaders take an audit of all the ministries and programs of his church. They analyze the effectiveness of each program in terms of evangelistic results and then classify them. The categories are (1) Nonessential and Nonproductive, (2) Essential but Nonproductive, and (3) Essential and Productive.

The ministries that fall into the category of Nonessential and Nonproductive are discontinued. When this church realized that Ingathering wasn't growing disciples or winning converts, they voted to discontinue it. There will always be ministries that move from Essential to Nonessential because the members no longer feel passionate about them. For example, a prison ministry that is being run out of a sense of obligation and tradition rather than a passion for the lost will cease to be an essential ministry because it is no longer productive.

Growing churches that have programs and/or ministries that are Essential but Nonproductive work to repurpose the ministries for evangelism. In one case, church leaders changed the primary focus of their Sabbath School classes from discussion to evangelism. When the Sabbath School leaders and teachers united around this concept, they invited seekers, used lessons that appealed to them, and developed an atmosphere that was conducive for evangelism.

The leaders of ministries that were found to be Essential and Productive worked to make those ministries even stronger. For instance, they recognized that the worship service was Essential and Productive but that it could be strengthened by gearing it more toward seekers. They launched an effort to provide an environment in which seekers could feel at home: they did away with churchy and Adventist jargon; they were careful to explain each element of the worship service; they selected songs that were easy to sing; and they made the sermons more practical and understandable.

The basic mission of our church will never change. However, our methodology and system need to be ever-changing, adapting to the shifting needs of people who don't know Jesus. The elements of the church's structure and system that don't contribute to the fulfillment of that mission can be eliminated to free up resources for the benefit of those that do work. Almost all the people my associates and I interviewed for our project agree that something needs to be changed. The basis of the structure should be one that supports mission.

Many years ago, a former General Conference president focused on the necessity of evaluating our system so we can make it a servant of our mission. He wrote, "Every level of church organization, from the congregation to the General Conference, exists solely to serve the mission of the church, not to perpetuate itself. . . . We must be driven by a vision of mission and not by policies carved in stone by people who lived under different circumstances."[13]

Using multiple ways to reach people is a matter of prioritizing and channeling all of the energy and resources of the church into expanding the kingdom of God. It will differ in each context according to the resources of the church and the needs of the community. Churches that strategically blend their approach to evangelism capitalize on the opportunities that open before them and allow the Holy Spirit to work through any and every way to lead people into a passionate relationship with God.

Though as members of the Seventh-day Adventist Church in North America we face significant challenges to the growth of our church, we can obtain valuable insights on how to overcome those challenges by learning from the churches that are growing. What we see there says that to be effective today, evangelism must include a focus on discipleship, an emphasis on relational evangelism, and the utilization of multiple ways of reaching people.

Jesus invites every believer to be a disciple of His, to share Him with their friends and family, and to unite with other believers to evangelize their community.

---

1. Daniel R. Sanchez, *Church Planting Movements in North America* (Fort Worth, Tex.: Church Starting Network, 2007), 18.

2. David Beckworth and S. Joseph Kidder, "Reflections on the Future of the Seventh-day Adventist Church in North America: Trends and Challenges," *Ministry* 82, no. 12 (December 2010): 20–22.

3. From 2003 to 2007, my research team and I studied Seventh-day Adventist churches in the North American Division (NAD) that were growing quite rapidly. We called all fifty-eight conferences within the NAD to identify churches that had sustained at least a 3 percent growth rate in attendance, membership, and baptisms for the previous three consecutive years. Congregations ministering to highly receptive first-generation immigrant communities were excluded. We identified twenty-three churches that met these criteria. In addition, for the purpose of comparison, we studied sixty-nine Adventist churches in the same geographical proximities that were plateauing or declining. The instruments of the research included a survey of attendees on Sabbath morning and personal interviews with pastors and focus groups.

4. For the full story of the powerful working of God to grow the churches I pastored, see S. Joseph Kidder, *The Big Four: Secrets to a Thriving Church Family* (Hagerstown, Md.: Review and Herald®, 2012).

5. Monte Sahlin, telephone interview, February 20, 2013.

6. Ron Gladden, *The 7 Habits of Highly Ineffective Churches* (Lincoln, Neb.: Advent Source, 2003), 49, 50.

7. In numerous seminars on public evangelism that I have attended, many cite the above statistic while a few suggest that one to three people attend for every one thousand handbills.

8. Thom S. Rainer, *The Unchurched Next Door* (Grand Rapids, Mich.: Zondervan, 2003), 24–26.

9. Ibid.

10. S. Joseph Kidder, "The Power of Relationships in Evangelism," *Ministry* 80, no. 7 (July 2008): 10–12.

11. Quoted by Elmer Towns in "Evangelism: Hot as Ever but Old Methods Are Cooling Off," *Fundamentalist Journal* (February 1984), 38.

12. For a description of the research, see endnote 3.

13. Robert S. Folkenberg, "Renewing Church Organization," *Adventist Review*, August 6, 1992, 15.

Chapter 4
Creating a Culture of Evangelism

"Him we proclaim, warning everyone and teaching everyone."—Colossians 1:28, ESV

"Brethren, do something; do something, do something! While committees waste their time over resolutions, do something. While Societies and Unions are making constitutions, let us win souls. Too often we discuss, and discuss, and discuss, and Satan laughs in his sleeve. It is time we had done planning and sought something to plan. I pray you, be men of action all of you. Get to work. . . . Our one aim is to save sinners, and this we are not to talk about, but to do in the power of God!"—C. H. Spurgeon[1]

What is the culture of your church? Are you apathetic or engaged? Is the focus on maintaining the status quo or on relevancy? What is your church's view regarding the condition of humanity? Does the culture of your weekly worship services and small groups invite people to "come as they are" and seek love, help, and healing? Do you know how to receive broken sinners in the midst of their pain, or does the culture of your church work against people admitting their hurts and faults until they are all better? Are you a "come and get clean" kind of church, or a place inviting only to the "already clean"?

I know, of course, that the business of grace and conversion belongs to the Holy Spirit, but it is our task as members to cooperate with the Spirit in order to stay useful for God's kingdom. I fear that many people in the church—even pastors and lay leaders—don't know how to create a culture that opens the door for the Spirit to work.

Leaders often ask what programs churches use to produce fully devoted disciples who are engaged in evangelism, ministry, worship, and hospitality. Specifically, they want to know how a church can become more evangelistic.

My answer points in a different direction than most people expect. I'm convinced that it's better for our churches to have an evangelistic culture than just to have a series of evangelistic programs. While there are a number of programs that reach some people, I find that both pastors and church members are dissatisfied because much of our evangelistic programming does very little to increase local church membership.[2] Churches with a program-driven approach to evangelism can restrict the sharing of the gospel to certain people at certain times. They may reserve it for the occasions when the evangelism team goes out visiting or when the church holds public evangelistic meetings.

Culture refers to the way of life of a group of people—the behaviors, beliefs, values, and symbols that they accept, generally without thinking about them, that are passed from one generation to the next by communication and imitation. In a church with an evangelistic culture, each member is encouraged to play a role in the congregation's effort to reach the people around the church with the message of salvation in Jesus. Every member works toward achieving this goal.

- Sabbath School classes will take on outreach projects.
- The entire congregation will pitch in to help support community children who attend church schools.
- The Sabbath School programs and worship services will be seeker-friendly.
- Women's ministries will knit scarves for the area homeless.
- Members will invite their neighbors to church socials and prayer breakfasts.
- Friday night Bible studies will begin with a fellowship meal.
- Potlucks will be filled with guests.
- The gym will be used for sports games that have been advertised in the local paper and that begin with a devotional time.
- The Pathfinder club will be composed of a mix of neighborhood and church kids.
- The members will host small group meetings in their homes or hold Bible studies or morning prayers at their workplaces.
- Regular seminars will address community needs—financial independence, marriage, divorce recovery—and will include invitations for nonmembers to worship with the members.

In other words, all the members will see evangelism and reaching the lost as part of their lifestyle. They'll all accept "Every one, win one" as their personal motto. They will want to know people individually and will strive to project an atmosphere of love, acceptance, and forgiveness. The heart of evangelism is taking the time to become acquainted with people as individuals so that we can see past stereotypes and imperfections and our ideal of what they should look like or how they should act. As we read the Gospels, we see that Jesus modeled this kind of acceptance. This is what drew the people who were most in need of love and forgiveness to Him.

In this chapter, I will introduce you to the tools, not programs, you can use to help your church fulfill its God-given calling and potential. With them, you can create in your church a culture that helps people grow in their love for the Lord and in their faithfulness at witnessing for Him. Here are the seven tools that will enable you to create an evangelistic culture in your church.

1. The gospel is the fuel of an evangelistic culture

The gospel message is the fuel that feeds an evangelistic culture in a church. We get excited about sports, food, and politics. If we want the members of our churches to be as excited about the gospel message, so they'll talk about it with non-Christians, then we need to help them fall deeply in love with Christ. That means they must understand the gospel message. It also means that the beauty of the gospel message must be put on display in our churches week in and week out. When Christians truly grasp the depth of their sin, the wonderful holiness of God, the perfection of Christ, the depth of His suffering for them, the power of His resurrection, and the gift of eternal life for all who repent and believe, then our love for and commitment to Christ will grow (see Colossians 3:1–17).

The gospel also frees Christians from motivations that might lead them to dislike evangelism. The gospel says we don't have to evangelize in order to earn God's love. Our position in God's family isn't dependent on how often or how well we share the gospel. We can be certain of God's love, which frees us from the overwhelming concern we would otherwise have about people's opinions of us that make us afraid to speak up about Jesus. Our role is to share Christ to the best of our ability. It is the job of the Holy Spirit to convict and to save. Many Christians hesitate to share the gospel with people close to them because they fear damaging their relationship. Remember, when people reject the gospel, they are rejecting God, not you, His messenger.

Center the church's weekly gatherings on the gospel. If the culture of kingdom citizenship depends on the gospel, then the church's weekly gatherings should be centered on the gospel. Every text should be preached with a view to exalt and honor Christ. The songs we sing should point to the Cross. We should confess our sinfulness in our corporate prayer, and then thank God for forgiveness.

2. Love and acceptance form the atmosphere of an evangelistic culture

Acceptance of the gospel will lead us to love and accept others regardless of who they are. The incident happened a few years ago, but I still remember it as clearly as if it happened yesterday. I was in the middle of a sermon. I can't recall much about the sermon except that I was pressing the point that God, in Jesus, was inviting us home. In making that point, I was talking about how it felt to be far away from home and desperate to get back. Right then, in the middle of my sermon, a woman rose to her feet and said loudly, "I want to come home!"

When I looked at her, I saw that she was weeping. Her husband was seated next to her, and his face bore a look of amazement and embarrassment. I stopped preaching, walked over to where she was, and put my arm around her. Then in a gentle voice, with her tears still streaming, she said, "I want to come home and have a relationship with God."

Right there, in the middle of the room, in the middle of the service, I asked everyone to join me, and I led her in prayer as she spoke directly to God about where she was in life and what she needed from Him. I encouraged her to trust in God's promises, and then we hugged and she sat down.

I don't remember whether or not I finished the sermon, but the story doesn't end there anyway. The following week I was with some of our longtime church members, and one of the women brought up what had happened on the previous Sabbath. I expected her to express the same joy that I had experienced, but I was sorely disappointed. Her comment was, "Things like that have no place in church." She went on to say, "That was awkward and embarrassing and out of order for a church worship service. Besides, I have more religion in my little finger than she has in her whole body."

I was shocked and didn't know how to respond. But then I was impressed to share with her Jesus' longing to embrace us rather than to condemn us as we anoint Him with overflowing worship and bathe His loving presence with our tears of repentance (John 8:1–11; 12:1–3).

I became convicted that I needed to use this experience to bring the congregation to an understanding that church is about love for one another. A church's culture can be changed through education and through modeling what loving God's children unconditionally looks like. So I preached a sermon series on love and acceptance. I spoke about the Samaritan woman whom Jesus asked for water, pointing out the reputation this woman had because she was known to be living with a man who wasn't her husband. Despite this woman's reputation, she was tasked with sharing the news of Christ's resurrection with the disciples, who were known to be quarrelsome.

I reminded the members of that church that Judas, the betrayer, ate in fellowship with Jesus at the Last Supper. And then there's the familiar story of the prodigal son. Though he was weary, though he smelled like pigs, and though he was ashamed of his failures, his father welcomed him home with open arms well before he made it to the house.

Don't be discouraged if you feel as though something's wrong with your church because of how long it's taking for the members to learn how to love. It took about five years of intentional preaching, education, prayer, and modeling for that church to step away from the culture that it had into a culture that promoted love, acceptance, and evangelism. Many people will leave a church that is judgmental and unloving, but few will leave a church home in which they feel accepted.

3. Prayer provides the power in an evangelistic culture

A church that is sharing the gospel must be committed to prayer. Evangelism seems to be a hopeless task. It means calling people who are dead spiritually to embrace life. How are we going to equip and encourage people to do that? It seems utterly futile.

> The Saviour knew that no argument, however logical, would melt hard hearts or break through the crust of worldliness and selfishness. He knew that His disciples must receive the heavenly endowment [the Holy Spirit]; that the gospel would be effective only as it was proclaimed by hearts made warm and lips made eloquent by a living knowledge of Him who is the way, the truth, and the life. The work committed to the disciples would require great efficiency, for the tide of evil ran deep and strong against them. A vigilant, determined leader was in command of the forces of darkness, and the followers of Christ could battle for the right only through the help that God, by His Spirit, would give them.[3]

In prayer, Christians go to the Lord confessing their insufficiency for the task of evangelism and pleading for the miracles that only He can perform. God alone can make the seeds that we sow spring up to eternal life in their hearts of those we're trying to reach.

Prayer is essential. Jesus said, "My house shall be called a house of prayer" (Matthew 21:13). Jesus didn't say, "My house shall be called a house of preaching" or "singing" or "fellowship"—although all of these are necessary. Jesus said, "My house shall be called a house of prayer" because it is only in prayer that hearts are softened and people are brought to the throne of grace.

We should pray for each other and for our loved ones not only on Sabbath mornings and evenings but every day of the week. We gather together as a congregation to pray that the Lord will spread His gospel through us. On Sabbath mornings people should share testimonies about the previous week and pray for opportunities to share the gospel in the coming week.

We must make certain our corporate prayers include our concern for the lost. Most church members aren't hesitant to pray for the physical needs of people. But less often do you see a church that prays together by name for those who aren't Christians. Often, when the church begins to pray for the lost in the community, God begins to answer those prayers in ways that make it clear that He's at work.

As we pray for the lost in our community, we must be sure that we offer our prayers from an attitude of concern rather than of condescension. The culture of the church becomes decidedly more evangelistic as the prayers of the members are infused with a burden for those who aren't followers of Jesus Christ.

Our corporate prayer time serves several purposes. First, we commit our-selves and our possessions to the Lord, asking for His blessing and direction. We should pray that we will behave with wisdom and tact toward those outside the church. We should also pray that we'll have opportunities for witnessing, and we should pray that we will give the right answers in every situation (Colossians 4:2–6; James 4:2b).

Praying corporately involves the whole church in the work of sharing the gospel. So, our witnessing isn't a task or a project that we undertake alone. Instead, we have brothers and sisters who will pray with us. This sharing makes it clear that evangelism is the work of "common" Christians. The people who are praying and those who are asking for prayer aren't, for the most part, pastors or elders or gifted evangelists. They are just believers who have embraced their calling to share the good news with the people around them.

This prayer time gets people off to a good start at reaching out to their neighbors and coworkers. If people are nervous or uncertain about sharing the good news, they should pray. They ask the Lord to give them opportunities—they ask Him to bring people who need the gospel to their attention. That's a much less in-timidating first step than rushing out with a tract in hand.

Finally, prayer makes us more loving and accepting. It softens our hearts and counteracts our innate prejudices. This makes us expect better relationships with the people in our sphere of influence. It opens up occasions for us to reach out to the people to whom we are witnessing.

One man who had tried for years to reach his daughter for Christ through reason and arguments became convicted of his need to pray instead. His prayers and the opening of his heart to God's work within him changed his life and attitudes. When his daughter noticed those changes, she wanted to learn more about the God who could transform him in that way. This brought them back into relationship with each other. And later this love relationship between the two of them brought the daughter to Jesus.

4. Training provides the blueprint for an evangelistic culture

Remember, our goal is for our churches to have an evangelistic culture rather than merely to run evangelistic programs. But that doesn't mean that there is no place for church leaders to organize and equip people to share the gospel. In fact, a love for the gospel and prayer will motivate Christians to want to be trained in ways of witnessing and of living a lifestyle of evangelism.

While evangelism will come naturally to some people in your congregation, there will be many others who love the gospel and pray faithfully but who still need to be equipped to share the gospel. In addition to the weekly sermon, you might offer seminars devoted to the topics that nurture the evangelistic culture. Train both your leaders and your members. Paul gave us a formula that has endured the test of time. "The things you have heard me say in the presence of many witnesses entrust to reliable people who will also be qualified to teach others" (2 Timothy 2:2). Paul trained Timothy, and Timothy trained the leaders in his churches, and those leaders trained the next generation. Many church members and even church leaders have never been equipped to help someone go from "lost" to "found." Devote time and resources to help your leaders find their own evangelistic voices. By following this example of Paul, I have been able to train as many as 150 teams in a church.

Talk openly and frequently about how to meet people where they are, how to give them spiritual comfort and hope, and how to lead them into a relationship with Jesus for eternity. Once the process and principles are clear, then your leaders can use the context and circumstances in the way that will best witness to each individual. I remember a church leader once saying to me that in all of his church experience he hadn't helped anyone to accept Jesus as Savior and Lord because he was never taught how to do so. How many of our leaders and church members feel woefully ill-prepared to meet people on their spiritual journeys and assist them to take the next step?

If ever there was a time to train our people how to reach out with the love of Jesus, it is now. I am convinced that if we can begin to create a culture of evangelism in all of our churches, our members will be equipped to minister to and be well received by this world, which is desperate for the love and redemption that only Christ can offer.

Here are a few ways church leaders can help their congregations:

- Train and equip one another. "Every church should be a training school for Christian workers."[4] Sabbath morning activities, Wednesday night prayer meetings, and small group programs can facilitate this training. Use all of the ministries and programs in the church to equip the members for evangelism. (See Ephesians 4:11ff.) Christians should gather for worship, fellowship, and training in order to learn how to put evangelism into practice every day of the week.
- Provide tools for evangelism and discipleship. In addition to the weekly sermon, you might offer Sabbath School classes devoted to these topics and recommend good books on the subject. Ellen G. White's *Evangelism* and her *Gospel Workers* are two of my favorites. Read these books with the people you are discipling, give them to people who will read them, and make them available through your church library.
- Always highlight testimonies of people who are doing wonderful things in the community through evangelism and ministry. Have them share what they've learned about what has worked and what hasn't. This encourages others and serves as an inspiration for them to do likewise.

- Bring people with you when you have a chance to share the gospel. As a pastor, I did my best to avoid doing ministry and evangelism alone. I always took people with me to train them to witness and share their faith or to bless the lives of others through their love and ministry. Make use of these opportunities to model for them how to share the good news.

- Address unbelievers in your sermons. Your people will learn and grow from listening to you engage people who don't know Jesus. Take time to consider thoughtfully the questions and objections that an unbeliever might have to your sermon's message, and then speak to those issues. If you preach to believers in your church, the seekers won't come and no one will invite them. If you speak to seekers and educate the believers that the church is to seek and save the lost, the believers will come, and they'll bring their friends.

- Conduct evangelistic meetings to which people can bring their friends and practice sharing the gospel. If your church can host an evangelistic café-style meeting or program, that will provide opportunities for your members to invite their friends and to observe and learn from you how to share the gospel.

- Also use seasonal days—Christmas, Easter, Mother's Day, and Thanksgiving—to build momentum in your church. Plan great worship services with meals to follow them. Print attractive cards advertising the event. Then give ten to twenty cards to each member and urge them to invite their friends to come.

   Advertise that a series of meetings will begin that day. Make it one that will be of interest to the unchurched, such as family relationships, how to raise kids, how to deal with finances, or how to have a better marriage. Spread the word during these meetings that on an upcoming Sabbath, you will answer the question as to whether Christianity works. On that Sabbath your attendance may well be 30 to 40 percent higher than usual, and the next Sabbath, while your attendance won't be that high, it will definitely be much larger than it was before. I go into this in much more detail in the chapter of this book titled "Planning a Sermonic Year."

- Begin a small-scale program of evangelistic mentoring. Asking a person to mentor someone else engenders accountability. I once mentored a new Christian named Steve, teaching him how to begin a conversation about Jesus. We worked together on the essential elements of a gospel presentation. At first we went together to talk with people who weren't Christians. Eventually, Steve became comfortable sharing Christ on his own, and over a three-year period he brought four people to Christ. He soon began mentoring others as I had mentored him.

5. Lifestyle is the heart of an evangelistic culture

In order to create a culture of evangelism, we need to think about helping people become disciples who love God passionately and obey Him wholeheartedly. Unbelievers will know we are Christ's disciples by our love for one another (see John 13:35).

Paul reminds us to live a lifestyle that is conducive to evangelism. In the letter he wrote to the believers in Ephesus, he said, "I urge you to live a life worthy of the calling you have received. Be completely humble and gentle; be patient, bearing with one another in love. Make every effort to keep the unity of the Spirit through the bond of peace" (Ephesians 4:1–3).

How do Christ-centered churches develop a culture of discipleship, evangelism, and mutual care? Paul admonishes that we are to "share with the Lord's people who are in need. Practice hospitality" (Romans 12:13). That's what citizens of Christ's kingdom do. We "live as citizens worthy of the gospel," which means "striving side by side for the faith of the gospel" (Philippians 1:27, my translation; cf. 3:20).

One of the churches I pastored hadn't seen one person become a Christian in the previous twenty-six years. Rather than complain to the congregation about their evangelistic ineptness, I began to pray for opportunities to be a witness for the gospel in the community. The results were amazing! I was surprised at how many doors God opened. I rejoiced over how many people responded positively to the gospel. And I was stunned by how many members of that church followed my example. In the year that followed, the church that hadn't seen a baptism in twenty-six years had eleven baptisms.

The way you carry yourself will tell others what a relationship with God can do. Carrying around a bad attitude not only drives people away from you, it also misrepresents the character of God. "Whatever is done to the glory of God is to be done with cheerfulness, not with sadness and gloom. There is nothing gloomy in the religion of Jesus. If Christians give the impression by a mournful attitude that they have been disappointed in their Lord, they misrepresent His character and put arguments into the mouth of His enemies. Though in words they may claim God as their Father, yet in gloom and sorrow they present to the world the aspect of orphans."[5]

So, show the world the joy that comes from knowing that Christ has accepted you—that you belong to Him.

Programs don't make lifestyles. Positive lifestyles are built of uplifting and supportive relationships that are founded on love and hospitality. But it's hard to construct relationships of that kind with people when our days are filled with jobs and chores and church duties and TV and the Internet. In fact, church members might have more time for discipling and evangelism if we canceled some of our programs and encouraged them to use those hours to develop the kind of schedule Jesus would have if He were in our place. Challenge the members to devote three or four hours every week in ministry to the community. And make sure there are social activities on the calendar that are welcoming to the unchurched.

6. Friendship is the glue of an evangelistic culture

Friendships are relationships in which people grow in their understanding of each other. A friend offers bread when you're hungry, a shoulder to cry on, a listening ear, and a push when you need it. Friendship is about rejoicing together over victories gained and providing support when things fall apart. It's bringing cookies and casseroles to your neighbors. It's building awareness of other people and seeing them with love as God does.

Learn how to pursue friends, family, coworkers, classmates, and roommates and share the gospel with them. Christians are usually less fearful of sharing the gospel with people they know than with people they don't know. Seventy-five percent of those who come to the Lord and the church come as a result of friendship evangelism.[6] Commit yourself to a continuing relationship with the people you are ministering to. From the first contact with someone to that person's commitment to Christ can be a matter of years—sometimes up to three years.[7] Most Christians would agree that they were exposed to the gospel through numerous modes and methods prior to their conversion.

Because unbelievers are exposed to the gospel through the everyday relationships and interactions they have with Christians, we are instructed to make the best use of our time around seekers, acting wisely, speaking graciously, and giving informed answers about the gospel (see Colossians 4:5, 6; see also 1 Peter 3:15, 16).

- Naaman, defying convention, was willing to seek out the prophet of God because of the recommendation of his wife's trustworthy slave girl (2 Kings 5:1–5).
- The Gerasene man went home and told his friends about the miracle he had experienced and how much Jesus had done for him (Mark 5:19, 20).
- Andrew brought his brother Peter to Jesus, and Philip brought his friend Nathanael, encouraging him to come and see what Jesus was doing (John 1:40–51).
- The Samaritan woman told her whole town about her encounter with Jesus because she found in Him the acceptance she had been searching for (John 4:28–42).

We are not to limit our association to fellow believers alone.

The example of Christ in linking Himself with the interests of humanity should be followed by all who preach His word, and by all who have received the gospel of His grace. We are not to renounce social communion. We should not seclude ourselves from others. In order to reach all classes, we must meet them where they are. They will seldom seek us of their own accord. Not alone from the pulpit are the hearts of men touched by divine truth. There is another field of labor, humbler, it may be, but fully as promising. It is found in the home of the lowly, and in the mansion of the great; at the hospitable board, and in gatherings for innocent social enjoyment.[8]

Don't be satisfied with confining the gospel proclamation to the church building. That places the burden upon the seeker of *coming to us* to hear the gospel message. Instead, we are to *go to them*, partaking in the joy and blessings that come with hearing and sharing the transformational gospel message.

7. Testimonies are the model and inspiration of an evangelistic culture

Create a culture ripe for evangelism through the regular use of testimonies. Even in a church where only twenty-five adult worshipers attend, there are enough stories to fill every other Sabbath service for an entire year. Start listening for stories that you know would be appropriate to share and that would increase the culture of evangelism. Each of us has a story of redemption, and hearing about God's work in our lives will touch someone who is listening.

Testimonies don't have to be reserved for church services to inspire others to live out an evangelistic culture. Tim was married to Michelle, a Christian woman, but he wasn't a Christian himself, and he wasn't interested in becoming one. Michelle spent much time telling him what she was learning about Jesus and praying for his heart to be softened.

Time passed, and Tim continued to go his own way. But then one Sabbath several years later, when Michelle entered the sanctuary, she was shocked to see Tim standing in the baptismal tank, ready to make the same commitment that Michelle had made. Years before, a church member had befriended Tim, and recently Tim had been studying with him because he wanted to know more about the Jesus his wife had been describing. Tim is one of many for whom conversion was a slow process rather than a quick 180-degree turn.

Just before her thirtieth birthday, Pam, who was raised in the church, was diagnosed with an aggressive form of cancer. For the seven years since then she has been working full-time while continuing treatments to help control the cancer. Even though her cancer continues to spread and it seems unlikely that she will experience remission, Pam lives her life with such joy that people are constantly commenting on her good spirits. She is often interviewed about how she can have such a positive outlook when she has a terminal disease. She is quick to credit God for blessing her with good friends, doctors, and employers and with a good support system in her church. Pam humbly asks for prayers during each treatment, and she shares with all who will listen the strength and encouragement they bring her. Stories like Pam's open up new ways for people to experience salvation and hope.

Generally, it's the people who have just come to Christ who have the widest circle of un-churched and de-churched friends. And often people are most passionate about things they've just learned. So people just coming to faith often make the best testimonies—they're still filled with the awe and excitement that comes from meeting Jesus. Be careful though—tapping into their passion and witness could lead to revival!

A culture of evangelism involves both spiritual renewal and intentionality in all areas of your life. There is no program that can create an evangelistic culture in your church. Developing one will require church leaders to teach, model, and pray until members of the church realize that sharing the gospel is their privilege and responsibility. A church with such a culture will be far more fruitful than a church without it—even if it's loaded with effective programs and strategies. We want evangelism to become the normative experience of every believer and for them to share the gospel in the context of their everyday relationships.

---

1. Charles H. Spurgeon, *Lectures to My Students: A Selection From Addresses Delivered to the Students of the Pastors' College, Metropolitan Tabernacle,* vol. 2 (Ulan Press, 2011), 65, 66.

2. Even with a renewed focus on evangelism and a push for evangelistic programs over the past few years, the North American Division of the Seventh-day Adventist Church had membership growth of only 1.5 percent from 2012 to 2013, as per the *2014 Annual Statistical Report,* found at http://www.adventiststatistics.org/ (accessed August 21, 2014).

3. White, *Acts of the Apostles,* 31.

4. Ellen G. White, *Ministry of Healing,* (Mountain View, Calif: Pacific Press®, 1942), 149.

5. Ellen G. White, *Thoughts From the Mount of Blessing* (Mountain View, Calif: Pacific Press®, 1896), 88.

6. Kidder, *The Big Four,* 116.

7. Internet Evangelism Day, "Jesus' Methods: Befriending and Relationships," accessed May 6, 2014, http://www.internetevangelismday.com/relationships.php.

8. Ellen G. White, *The Desire of Ages* (Mountain View, Calif.: Pacific Press®, 1940), 152.

Chapter 5
Jesus' Way of Reaching the Unchurched

"Jesus went through all the towns and villages, teaching in their synagogues, proclaiming the good news of the kingdom and healing every disease and sickness. When he saw the crowds, he had compassion on them, because they were harassed and helpless, like sheep without a shepherd. Then he said to his disciples, 'The harvest is plentiful but the workers are few. Ask the Lord of the harvest, therefore, to send out workers into his harvest field.'"—Matthew 9:35–38

"Christ's method alone will give true success in reaching the people. The Saviour mingled with men as one who desired their good. He showed His sympathy for them, ministered to their needs, and won their confidence. Then He bade them, 'Follow Me.' There is need of coming close to the people by personal effort. If less time were given to sermonizing, and more time were spent in personal ministry, greater results would be seen. The poor are to be relieved, the sick cared for, the sorrowing and the bereaved comforted, the ignorant instructed, the inexperienced counseled. We are to weep with those that weep, and rejoice with those that rejoice. Accompanied by the power of persuasion, the power of prayer, the power of the love of God, this work will not, cannot, be without fruit."—Ellen G. White[1]

Jesus compared the people of this world to grain that is ripe and plentiful and then asked His disciples to pray for more people to be involved in reaping the "grain." Christians have tried to follow Jesus' instructions. For generations they have sought ways of connecting the unchurched with the saving power of Christ, yet they've been less than successful: fewer than one-third of the world's population identify themselves as Christian,[2] and that figure hasn't changed much in the past one hundred years[3]—in fact, church attendance is on the decline.

You might guess that Christians have done better in America, but recent research has shown that less than 20 percent of Americans attend church on a regular or semi-regular basis.[4] This means there are 252 million unchurched people in this country, making it the third most unchurched nation in the world. In other words, the majority of the people in your community don't consider themselves to be members of any church. Consequently, the traditional methods of evangelism—which generally involved asking the unchurched to attend meetings conducted in a church—are having less of a response today. So the question is, what can we do to increase the impact our witnessing has on the unchurched?

If we truly want to draw people to the kingdom, we need to embrace Christ's way of reaching them. "The Saviour mingled with men as one who desired their good [Luke 15:1, 2]. He showed His sympathy for them [John 8:1–11], ministered to their needs [Mark 2:1–12], and won their confidence [John 9:1–12]. Then He bade them, 'Follow Me.' [Matthew 11:28–30]."[5]

Christ actively sought people who were spiritually "ripe"; He didn't wait for them to find Him. We believe that the message of Christ is still relevant some two thousand years after His death. His approach for sharing that message is just as relevant today. Let's see how He reached out to the people in His community.

Reaching the unchurched

How do we create a lifestyle and culture that minister to the people around us as Jesus ministered to those He met? Jesus did more healing and socializing than preaching. The atmosphere around Him was one of hope, value, and forgiveness. "That God would enter into this world as human is an amazing truth. But that was His communication strategy. His presence here made all the difference. He was not sending a word, He *was* the Word to man. . . . In the same way, the Christian community in the world not only carries that message, we *are* a message. We are a living demonstration of the reality of God in a fallen world."[6]

Like the people whom Jesus met in the flesh, the unchurched people of today desire these feelings of hope, value, and forgiveness. Jesus has called the church body to be His hands today—reaching out and touching those who are hurting. Here are five steps toward implementing the evangelistic example Jesus gave to us.

1. Pray for the unchurched

Prayer should permeate all of our efforts to evangelize. Scripture assures us that God is at work redeeming the world. Jesus wept and prayed over the spiritual condition of the city of Jerusalem (see Luke 19:41). He wants us to be sensitive to His activity around us.

Make it your habit, your practice, to pray for your neighbors, family members, coworkers, and acquaintances in the community. Pray for them by name. Pray that you will be open for opportunities to share the gospel. Prayer shouldn't be a mere minute-long mention of our concern. Instead, we should provide opportunities for members to pray earnestly for the evangelism efforts of the church.

Establish prayer groups that meet for the sole purpose of praying for the unchurched in your community. Make the midweek prayer service more than merely time to read a list of those who are sick; make it truly a time for the church to pray for God to work where you live—for Him to bless your evangelistic activities. Jesus prayed not only for the unity of His disciples but also for those who would hear the message that they, too, might believe and be saved (John 17:20–23).

Every year I pray that God will lead me to five people whom I can introduce to Him that year, and I always request what I call evangelistic eyes. The Lord has never failed. In each of the fourteen years since I started to pray for these specific things, I've never had fewer than seven baptisms, and one year I baptized thirty-six.

Recently, my wife and I were invited to a birthday party for one of the members of our church. When we arrived, I noticed that while most of the guests had found someone to talk to, one couple were by themselves. So I decided to talk with them.

The couple told me they were neighbors of the man whose birthday we were celebrating. Since everyone else went to the same church and these people didn't attend that church, they didn't know anyone else there, and no one had taken the initiative to talk with them.

I introduced myself and asked them about themselves. They told me that they weren't attending a church. While the husband had enjoyed going to church as a child, when he was on his own he had drifted away, and since then he hadn't found a church that appealed to him. His wife said her parents didn't attend religious services, and she had never been to one herself.

I told this couple a bit about myself and how I became a Christian. This interested the man, and he asked me to come to their home later that week to keep the discussion going. Of course, I said Yes, and I started to study the Bible with them. Before long this couple, who were living together but weren't married, decided to give their hearts to God. We had a beautiful ceremony in which they were joined to each other in marriage and joined to God through baptism.

2. Commit yourself to developing relationships with the unchurched

Here's a guideline that may sound like a cliché but is a good rule of thumb to keep in mind: don't invite people to your church until you have spent some time with them socially. In other words, get to know people at a meal or some other social event before you attempt to attempt to talk with them about God. Spend time getting acquainted. Find interests you share and can enjoy together. Ask them where they're from and what their spiritual background has been. Invite them to attend sporting or cultural events with you. Pray for them daily, and look for ways to minister to them, such as mowing their yard while they're on vacation or working on projects together. The apostle John pictures Jesus making those social connections with the Samaritan woman at the well (John 4:1–29). Helping the unchurched to become fully devoted followers of Jesus Christ is not a quick-strike operation. It requires a long-term commitment to the relationships you establish.

A few years ago I baptized a woman by the name of Sara. As was my practice, I visited her the Sunday after her baptism to cast the vision for her of reaching out to her family with the love of God. While I was there, I noticed that every wall in her house was covered with pictures of fish and of her husband, Roger, with his catch of the day.

Roger was an avid fisherman who had a boat with a state-of-the-art sonar fish finder. He went fishing two or three times a week. So I realized that if I really wanted to reach this man's heart, I'd better learn everything I could about fishing. I started to read everything I could about fishing. I also started to visit Roger once or twice a week, and we talked about fishing. Then one day I asked Roger if I could go fishing with him and bring my son with me. Roger was delighted to take us with him.

During the week before our expedition I prayed that God would do something unusual that day. I didn't know what to ask for other than that it be a miracle.

The day of our trip, we spent about five hours on a lake. It was an amazingly beautiful day, and my son and I had a great time. At the end of the day, we counted our catch. My son had caught two fish and I had caught seven big ones, but Roger hadn't caught any. This embarrassed and upset him. He asked, "How did you do that? This is your first day fishing!" I said, "I prayed about it." And then Roger said, "Teach me about prayer." A few months later he was baptized.

To reach the people God brings your way, you might have to learn to fish or crochet, to repair cars or to cook. Developing relationships that lead to spiritual commitments will most likely require you to get out of your comfort zone. But those relationships open people up to spiritual growth.

3. Meet the needs of the unchurched

The unchurched may or may not be concerned about the doctrinal stands of your church. Many don't care what version of the Bible you read or how your church is governed. Most of them are drowning in the whirlpool of life's realities, and they don't believe the church can do anything to help them. While they are open to spiritual things, experiencing faith in a church setting has been a stumbling block.

Their concerns are more pragmatic: finding a job that pays well, meeting their mortgage payments, putting food on the table, getting out of debt, maintaining job security. They're stressed about their health and family matters.

They'd appreciate help with child-rearing: discipline, school events, dating, and allowances. Single parents worry about how to carry the load alone. Many adults are concerned with the challenges of meeting the needs of aging parents. And they want close personal friendships and a clear purpose for living.

Jesus always spoke to the needs of the individual. Whether it was the woman at the well or the blind man by the pool of Siloam, He met people where they were, and He gave them comfort and hope for the future. He invites everyone: "Come to me, all you who are weary and burdened, and I will give you rest. Take my yoke upon you and learn from me, for I am gentle and humble in heart, and you will find rest for your souls. For my yoke is easy and my burden is light" (Matthew 11:28–30).

Jesus also said, "It is not the healthy who need a doctor, but the sick. . . . I have not come to call the righteous, but sinners" (Matthew 9:12, 13). Churches that reach their communities embody the doctrine of grace. When people's lives have been changed, they share that good news with others who are seeking hope, help, and healing. Ellen G. White wrote of what Jesus did:

> During His ministry, Jesus devoted more time to healing the sick than to preaching. His miracles testified to the truth of His words, that He came not to destroy, but to save. Wherever He went, the tidings of His mercy preceded Him. Where He had passed, the objects of His compassion were rejoicing in health and making trial of their new-found powers. Crowds were collecting around them to hear from their lips the works that the Lord had wrought. His voice was the first sound that many had ever heard, His name the first word they had ever spoken, His face the first they had ever looked upon. Why should they not love Jesus and sound His praise? As He passed through the towns and cities He was like a vital current, diffusing life and joy.[7]

Jesus' model of practical Christianity is about relieving the burdens of others. Examine your church. Bible study must go beyond what happened thousands of years ago among a group of nomads wandering in the desert. It must be directed toward application to people's lives now so God can transform them.

If the church is going to make a difference, it must become like Jesus in His love and grace and redeeming power. When church is done right, it is a place of grace and hope that God uses to change people and make the world better.

Jesus embodied the prophecy of Isaiah,

"The Spirit of the Lord is on me,
    because he has anointed me
    to proclaim good news to the poor.

He has sent me to proclaim freedom for the prisoners
　　and recovery of sight for the blind,
　to set the oppressed free,
　　to proclaim the year of the Lord's favor"
　　　　(Luke 4:18, 19; see also Isaiah 61:1, 2).

Consider starting community family groups that meet in apartment buildings or in homes. Use these groups to address life issues from a biblical perspective. Provide useful answers and tools. Show how God is helping struggling church members as a testimony to what He can do for the unchurched too. Find ways in which you can become God's eyes, seeing hurting people, and His hands, extending hope and joy and acceptance to the needy.

4. Make your church seeker-friendly

Reaching the unchurched will require you to leave your comfort zone. You will need to begin by looking at your church through the eyes of a seeker. Take the time to view your church service and environment from the viewpoint of someone who has never been to a church before.

Reaching the unchurched may require us to change how we do some things. These people aren't familiar with the language, practice, or culture of your church. Many have told me that stepping into a church is like stepping into a foreign country. Make sure that what is said from the pulpit and in the church bulletins and other means of communication comes in language that everyone understands. Jesus is known for His use of simple language and object lessons that are easy to understand and to identify with. Add descriptions regarding the various elements of the service to help those new to the experience to understand the meaning behind them. If there are practices that have no meaning, consider modifying or eliminating them.

Avoid the use of Adventist jargon such as "NAD," "stewardship," and "Spirit of Prophecy." Be sure to explain the meaning of historically Christian doctrines such as sanctification and justification. Don't assume that everyone listening understands the meaning of these words and phrases.

Encourage the members of your church to avoid cliquish grouping between services and at potlucks. Make a concerted effort as a church to interact with all the visitors. And beware of any local traditions that may make seekers uncomfortable or embarrassed, such as having all the visitors stand and introduce themselves.

While modifying or eliminating practices such as these isn't always easy, it's necessary so that the unchurched will feel comfortable enough in your church to want to return. Make it a regular practice to review your church and its services from the viewpoint of the seeker.

5. Promote a sense of acceptance

Remember that most seekers are looking to experience something bigger than themselves. They want to belong somewhere. Yet most churches tend to follow the formula that says Believing + Behaving → Belonging.[8] If you believe like us and you behave the way we behave—you talk, eat, and dress like us—then you can belong in our community.

Historically, evangelism has begun with the sharing of knowledge—that is, with our beliefs. We use the Bible to show to the unchurched the truth of the Sabbath, hoping that the Holy Spirit will convict them regarding this biblical truth and that they will keep the Sabbath. It is only when they have accepted the Sabbath and our other distinctive doctrines that we show them experientially what it feels like to belong to our church community.

While this method still works for some, I suggest a different paradigm—one that fosters a sense of belonging that provides a foundation on which all our beliefs can stand. In this approach, the first presentation of several on the topic of the Sabbath isn't a sermon or even a Bible study. Instead, it consists of your sharing Sabbath afternoons with the friends to whom you are introducing the Sabbath. You invite them over for lunch, you take them on nature hikes, and maybe you even invite them to attend church services with you.

At some point in this process they will have noticed the joy and peace the Sabbath brings to you, and they will have begun to experience it for themselves too. This will lead them to ask about the principles and beliefs that guide your understanding of the Sabbath. That gives you the opportunity to share with them from the Bible the truth of the Sabbath. Because they have already experienced what the Sabbath can do for them, they are likely to have felt convicted of its biblical truth before you even present it formally. When we start with belonging and then move to behaving, believing will follow.

Postmoderns are looking for a community to which they can belong. Once they feel accepted for who they are, they are more open to changing their values and beliefs. When they understand what God is calling them to be and do, they will change their behavior. Find ways to develop your church culture into one in which everyone feels that they belong.

Acceptance is what people are looking for. God wants you to accept others in the same way that Jesus accepted you. He has an unconditional love for all, regardless of who they are. In faith, we delight in God's acceptance of us when we were unacceptable, and we demonstrate our love of Him by freely offering the same gift to others. We set aside our prejudices and judgments in order to see what eyes have not seen and hear what ears cannot hear (1 Corinthians 2:9) so we can comfort those in need. God's love allows us to offer a sense of belonging to those who haven't even realized they're in need of it.

The unchurched want to know whether Christianity will work for them.

They ask, "Does following Jesus make any difference in *your* life?" "Does the Bible have anything to say about *my* problems?" How you answer these questions will influence how receptive they are of the gospel.

Let your life demonstrate the practical aspects of a walk with God. Address the hot buttons that trouble the unchurched. Talk about these issues outside of the walls of the church. The argument today is not about whether Christianity is real; it is whether Christianity works. Let your life be the answer, showing that a relationship with Christ not only works but makes life worth living.

Christ's way of reaching people begins with touching their lives by meeting their needs and making them whole. It culminates with Jesus calling them to follow Him so they can have a relationship with Him. That is our mission today.

---

1. White, *The Ministry of Healing*, 143.

2. "The Global Religious Landscape," Pew Research Center, December 18, 2012, http://www .pewforum.org/2012/12/18/global-religious-landscape-exec/.

3. "Global Christianity—A Report on the Size and Distribution of the World's Christian Population," Pew Research Center, December 19, 2011, http://www.pewforum.org/2011/12/19 /global-christianity-exec/.

4. Rebecca Barnes and Lindy Lowry, "7 Startling Facts: An Up Close Look at Church Attendance in America," ChurchLeaders, accessed May 7, 2014, http://www.churchleaders.com/pastors/pastor -articles/139575-7-startling-facts-an-up-close-look-at-church-attendance-in-america.html.

5. White, *The Ministry of Healing*, 143.

6. Wayne McDill, *Making Friends for Christ: A Practical Approach to Relational Evangelism*, 2nd ed. (Xulon Press, 2010), 22.

7. White, *The Ministry of Healing*, 19, 20.

8. For further explanation, see Richard Rice, *Believing, Behaving, Belonging: Finding New Love for the Church* (Roseville, Calif.: Association of Adventist Forums, 2002).

Chapter 6
Friendship Evangelism[1]

"Keep on loving one another as brothers and sisters. Do not forget to show hospitality to strangers."—Hebrews 13:1, 2

What causes people to decide to give their hearts to Jesus? Is it evangelistic meetings? Bible studies? Social events? Acts of kindness? Relationships? Do special circumstances bring it about, or does it take place among the ordinary events of life? As you read the following story, try to identify the key influence that led Bobbie to give her life completely to Jesus and to join the Adventist Church.

When Bobbie Moersch left home at the age of eighteen, she had little interest in God. But after she married and had children, she began attending the Methodist church, though her visits were only occasional because her husband's work required them to move frequently.

Bobbie raised and sold poodles. In the mid-1990s, she and her husband were living in Niles, Michigan. Kathy Herbel, a Seventh-day Adventist, came to Bobbie's home to buy a poodle puppy. But Bobbie had already sold all the puppies from the most recent litter. However, because Bobbie had such a good reputation as a breeder, Kathy decided that rather than buying a puppy elsewhere, she would wait until she could get one from Bobbie. While the Herbels waited, they visited Bobbie frequently to see how "mama's" pregnancy was progressing. Eventually, the puppies were born and the Herbels chose the one they wanted—an apricot miniature poodle that they named Cider. But that time of waiting resulted in more than just the purchase of a puppy. It also started a friendship that now spans more than two decades.

The strength of a relationship is measured by what one's friends are willing to do to help you. By that measure, the Herbels' relationship with Bobbie is a strong one. For instance, when Kathy stopped by Bobbie's home one day, she noticed a pile of fencing in the driveway. Obviously, Bobbie wanted a fence raised. But she couldn't erect that fence by herself, and her husband wasn't able to help her because he had Alzheimer's. Seeing Bobbie's need, Kathy drew members from the Niles church and from another local Adventist church and got that fence installed. Good friends help one another even though it costs time and energy.

Through the years the Herbels frequently invited Bobbie and her husband to special programs and other activities that were held at the Niles church. Sometimes the Moersches accepted their invitation and attended special events there, including several evangelistic meetings. During the appeals made at those meetings, Kathy prayed for Bobbie, knowing that she was wrestling with conviction. Kathy was certain that Bobbie would surrender herself to Jesus, but Bobbie resisted.

Sisters in suffering

In April 2001, Bobbie's husband died. Bobbie reacted by becoming angry and turning away from God. The Herbels continued to invite her to church, but Bobbie used her many health problems as an excuse for staying away. She tended to isolate herself in such circumstances, but Kathy and her mother, LeAnne, maintained the connection with her, always praying for her and helping her whenever they could. Kathy, who was a nurse, at times served almost as a private nurse for her friend.

Bobbie had always considered pushy, aggressive Christians to be a turnoff, but the Herbels were gentle and loving in their witness to Bobbie. In fact, the discussions they'd had when they first met her weren't overtly spiritual. Yet even back then, Bobbie had somehow sensed that they were Christians. Now, Kathy and LeAnne continued to pray with Bobbie and to visit her during her illnesses—and their relationship became very close—similar to what mothers and daughters experience. Bobbie felt comfortable opening her heart to Kathy and LeAnne. She called LeAnne "my angel," because her prayers and words of encouragement were so powerful. These spiritual nudges came naturally and sincerely.

Kathy and LeAnne were supportive when Bobbie's husband died. And Kathy experienced some significant personal losses at that time, which drew the two women even closer together as they supported and encouraged each other. Kathy became acquainted with Bobbie's extended family and even joined Bobbie and her two daughters on a cruise.

Finally, progress

Late in 2003, Bobbie started coming to the Adventist church in Niles. Seven years later, as she was sitting by herself and watching the families enjoying the fun and games at the fall festival the church held in the gymnasium of the school, the love, friendship, and sense of family and belonging that she saw in the church members overwhelmed her. Speaking out loud but to no one in particular, she said, "I want to be part of this!" The relational warmth that she saw at the church made her want to become a member.

A little while later Bobbie was in a hospital, and Kathy and LeAnne dropped by to visit her. During that visit, Kathy asked Bobbie whether she would like to join the Niles church. Bobbie said Yes, she had made up her mind to do just that. And when she was home again, she began to attend the Niles church regularly. What joy and happiness this brought to the hearts of Kathy and LeAnne!

Soon after this, Bill Dudgeon, the associate pastor, asked Bobbie whether she wanted to take Bible studies, not knowing that she had already decided to be baptized. She found these sessions—in which she learned more about the Jesus who had loved her and cared for her all those years—to be precious. And on the last day of 2011, Bobbie was baptized and became a member of the Niles Westside Seventh-day Adventist Church. So God used a poodle, patience, prayer, social activity, and the Word to bring Bobbie to salvation.

Now, back to our question. What was the one key influence that caused Bobbie to give her heart to the Lord and to join the Niles church? The answer is that there wasn't one—there were at least four influences that brought her to the moment of decision: the numerous answers to prayer for healing, the loving witness of the Herbel family through the years, the social activities that drew her close to other members of the church, and the understanding of truth given her in the evangelistic meetings she attended and through the Bible studies she had. Evangelism isn't a matter of a single approach or event that brings people to the Lord. It's all the many influences that create the atmosphere that gradually moves people toward God.

Lessons learned

Here are a few imperatives of evangelism that we can draw from Bobbie's story and that research has confirmed.

1. Seize opportunities. God used the search for a poodle to connect believers with a seeker. We all need to look for opportunities to begin a relationship with someone. Pray that God will reveal to you where He is working. Jesus used His thirst to break the barriers between Him and the Samaritan woman at the well (John 4). He used Nicodemus's curiosity as a path that led that Jewish leader to friendship with the Savior (John 3). Paul even used idols to bridge the divide between him and the Athenians (Acts 17). Pray that the Lord will give you clear eyesight to recognize openings for relationship that can lead people to Jesus. The Holy Spirit can use a well, a cup of water, a pagan idol, and even the purchase of a poodle to reach hearts!

2. Be intentional. Build relationships with people as a means of eventually leading them to Jesus. Socialize with them. Love them. Meet their needs. Invest your life in them. The Herbel family didn't just get to know Bobbie casually; rather, they gently and authentically loved her. When she was in the hospital, they visited her. When she lost her husband, they grieved with her and comforted her. When she was hurting, they cried with her and were available to her. When she was happy, they rejoiced with her. And they always kept her in their prayers.

3. Be patient and persistent. Most relationships don't develop quickly. They require time, effort, and purposefulness. One Web site on evangelism indicates that our outreach should not primarily be "cut and run." The fruit of evangelism usually doesn't mature overnight. A piece of literature isn't enough. According to Ed Stetzer, nonrelational evangelism is an oxymoron.[2] In several studies of how much time is required on average for the conversion of the typical adult, the participants have reported in retrospect the following observations:

- On average, there was a period of about three years during which they were in the process of inquiry.
- In more than 60 percent of conversions, a serious life problem played a large part in starting them on the journey.
- In more than 70 percent of conversions, a relationship with a Christian who was praying for them was the strongest factor—far more significant than watching videos or reading tracts, books, or even the Bible. They wanted what they saw modeled in the lives of their Christian friends.
- The majority of conversions ultimately took place in the context of church fellowship rather than in isolation.[3]

This suggests that any mode of evangelism that doesn't aim to draw people into real, trusting relationships with Christians is unlikely to be very fruitful. And since such relationships can be costly and time-consuming, Christians must be committed to living a life of faithfulness, authenticity, and integrity, and to intentionally share Jesus with others through deeds and words.

What being authentic means

The Holy Spirit will tell you when it's appropriate for you to share your story. The Herbels listened to the Spirit. They lived their faith with joy and commitment. They openly talked about faith and church. Jesus had done so much for them that they were anxious to tell their story to others in need.

Here are some ideas that might help you become more effective at sharing your faith:

- Make it clear in the course of your conversation that you are a Christian. Include in your conversation statements that are appropriate to the topic

and are based on God's Word.
- Don't hesitate to speak of the special benefits and blessings of being a Christian.
- When appropriate, give God the glory as you discuss good things that you experience—but avoid excessive praise, which can sound artificial and hypocritical.
- Don't try to tell people everything there is to know about Christianity all at once.
- Ask questions. Seek first to understand, and then to be understood. Make it a dialog.
- Be sensitive to their reactions; place yourself in their shoes.
- As you share your faith, seek wisdom from God through prayer. (See James 1:5; Nehemiah 2:4.)
- When you're asked to explain the plan of salvation, do so simply and clearly. (See Acts 18:24–26.)

Bear in mind that your purpose is not to convert; you are simply sharing your relationship with Jesus. The time for formal teaching will come later.

Invite them to church

Whenever possible, invite your friends to church activities. The best place to start is to invite them to accompany you to a nonthreatening social gathering. It was at a social gathering that Bobbie came to feel at home with the Niles church family and decided to become a part of it. It is also important to note that the Herbels weren't embarrassed to bring their friend to Sabbath School and to the worship service. The role of the church is to provide a safe and enjoyable place for people to bring their friends. This will help both prospective believers and new believers to feel that they belong even while they're becoming acquainted with other believers.

Here are some suggested activities:

- Include believers in the social, recreational, and work activities to which you invite your non-Christian friends.
- Invite your unchurched neighbors and friends to events at your church (worship, prayer meeting, socials, etc.).
- Invite them to Bible studies in someone's home. Include both Christians and non-Christians.
- Invite them to evangelistic meetings, group Bible studies, and small group meetings.

Be patient

The time it took Bobbie Moersch to choose to give herself to Jesus wasn't a matter of days or weeks or months. Sixteen years passed between the Herbels' first contact with her and her baptism. Some people will make a decision very quickly, but others will take more time. We must never give up on them. Even Jesus had to be patient. It took Nicodemus more than three years to reveal in public his belief in Jesus.

When we interviewed the Herbels, it became clear to us that prayer played a major role in the conversion of their friend Bobbie. They prayed for her salvation, her healing, her husband, and her general well-being. The Herbels never viewed Bobbie as an object; they saw her as a friend whom they loved and appreciated deeply.

Jesus prayed for people to be saved and to be healed. Some were grateful and no doubt became part of His band of followers. Healing prayer seemed to be a gateway for the message Jesus brought. Trust increased, and people were prepared to hear the message of the kingdom. Jesus wants to use us to bring hope, peace, and purpose to the people in our sphere of influence.

Both public and relational evangelism work. Even shopping for a poodle can become an opportunity to do evangelism. Imagine what would happen if you started to share your faith with people in your sphere of influence: family, friends, and colleagues. Picture your children in the kingdom of God, enjoying Jesus for eternity because you were serious about your faith. Consider how it would feel to have your mom and dad with you in heaven. Wouldn't it be great to enjoy eternity with your neighbors and colleagues? View people as God's precious children. Imagine your friends coming to you in heaven and saying, "I'm here because of you. Thank you!"

---

1. David Penno, associate professor at the Seventh-day Adventist Theological Seminary, assisted in the writing of this chapter.

2. "Jesus' Methods: Befriending and Relationships," Internet Evangelism Day, accessed April 12, 2012, http://www.internetevangelismday.com/relationships.php.

3. Ibid.

Chapter 7
Seeing What God Sees

"Day after day, in the temple courts and from house to house, they never stopped teaching and proclaiming the good news that Jesus is the Messiah."
—*Acts 5:42*

When I was a pastor, I felt very strongly that we should consider every-where we go, live, and work to be places where we can minister. I made it a point to visit the members of my church in their homes and workplaces and to challenge them to live lives of service and evangelism. By this I didn't mean that they all had to become pastors. Rather, I said that God asks all of us to minister through our careers.

For instance, there was Owen. He was a physician, and he owned his own clinic and had two other doctors who worked for him. I asked Owen to show me his clinic and tell me about what he does there. When we had spent about forty-five minutes visiting, I asked Owen whether we could dedicate his clinic to the glory of God. He said Yes, so I prayed.

When I finished my prayer, I said, "Owen, you are a Christian physician. Other doctors deal only with their patients' physical health, but *you* can also be concerned about their eternal salvation. God has called you to minister to people's spiritual needs as well as to their physical needs. I challenge you to pray for your patients, share your faith with them, and if possible, invite them to church or Bible study or any other spiritual function that you think would be appropriate."

Owen looked like he was shocked. He said that he had been a Christian all his life and was the son of a pastor, but he'd never thought about his work life that way before. Owen's reaction to my prayer showed me that many people don't think of their workplaces as sites for ministry.

Soon after I prayed for Owen and his clinic, he began to tell me exciting stories about what happened when he told his patients about God's power to heal and offered to pray for them and even brought them to church with him.

Owen was seeing his work in a different light. Now he realized it did more than merely provide the stability he and his family needed. It now also gave him a deeper purpose—that of helping his patients spiritually.

God has called every physician, every janitor, every CEO, every engineer—all of us—to serve as His ambassadors at all times and in all places. He challenges us to reach beyond the bounds of our professions to minister wherever we are.

Dare to be a Daniel

Daniel is a great example of living one's ministry. He worked hard at his profession, and he did a good job. The book of Daniel tells us what Daniel's coworkers thought of him. King Nebuchadnezzar said, "How great are [God's] signs, how mighty his wonders! His kingdom is an eternal kingdom, his dominion endures from generation to generation" (Daniel 4:3). What a testimony from a man who ruled an empire filled with gods! Daniel lived and breathed his relationship with God on a second-by-second basis. That's why people saw God in him. Because of his integrity and faith, people were in awe of his God.

Daniel lived with such integrity that King Darius planned to put him in control of the whole Persian Empire. This made his peers extremely jealous. They knew that Daniel's work was impeccable and that they'd find no grounds there that they could use to get him fired. So they tried to use Daniel's faith against him instead.

Through Daniel, King Darius had come to respect the power of Daniel's God, so now he implored Daniel to reach out to his God for rescue (see Daniel 6:16). When God did save Daniel from certain death, King Darius testified of His greatness to the entire kingdom, issuing a decree that "in every part of my kingdom people must fear and reverence the God of Daniel.

> "For he is the living God
> and he endures forever;
> his kingdom will not be destroyed,
> his dominion will never end.
> He rescues and he saves;
> he performs signs and wonders
> in the heavens and on the earth.
> He has rescued Daniel
> from the power of the lions"
> (Daniel 6:26, 27).

The life that Daniel lived revealed a character so strong and trustworthy that it impelled his coworkers and supervisors to testify to the greatness of his God. This kind of witness has not been restricted to Bible times alone. Take Lois for instance. She is becoming a chaplain as a second career. She recently told me that the goodness of God has been made so apparent by what He's doing in her life that her friends are telling their coworkers about it.

Luke says that Jesus drew sinners to Himself (see, for example, Luke 7:34; 15:1). Lois has this gift of "presence": God can use her as His hands to soothe those who are hurting. Lois can relate to people in all walks of life. She doesn't have to preach her faith formally; it's on display for all to see in what she does every day. She's a shoulder to cry on, a motivator, and a helping hand. And because of the friendship that she extends to the people around her and the view of God she shares with them, many people who haven't set foot inside a church for years attempt to convince their unchurched friends that the acceptance they feel from Lois is a reflection of the love and concern God has for all of His children.

Paul reminds us that we are called to live for God in *everything* that we do (1 Corinthians 10:31). We aren't to reflect God's glory only during the times when we're officially "on duty" as Christians. Paul told the Philippians, "*Whatever* happens, conduct yourselves in a manner worthy of the gospel of Christ" (Philippians 1:27; emphasis added). It seems that knowing what Christ has done for us should make us joyful and we would want to share the good news with others—not because we're obligated to do so, but because we *want* to tell others how much God has given us.

When the purpose of your life is to give glory to God, you won't have to struggle to evangelize. You'll do it automatically. When you are living for Christ, people will be attracted to what they see God doing in your life. They will be drawn to you and want to know what brings you such personal and spiritual fulfillment.

Through God's eyes

Once we as individuals realize that everything we do in life is a form of ministry, our perspective changes. We see people through the eyes of our Father in heaven, and then our communities and places of work become places where we can witness to others about our loving God. Then business and profit take second place to our concern about the spiritual needs of the people with whom we work. Then we'll see our coworkers as people who are in need of a Savior.

God gives us His eyes so we can see the world and reach others. It isn't social status that moves God; it's the pain His children are experiencing. Matthew, who was there, wrote, "When [Jesus] saw the crowds, he had compassion on them, because they were harassed and helpless, like sheep without a shepherd" (Matthew 9:36).

- Jesus saw Jairus's grief, and He raised his daughter from the dead (Luke 8:40–56).

- Jesus saw the Samaritan woman at the well, and He offered her living water (John 4:1–30).
- Jesus saw a woman consumed by guilt, and He forgave her (John 8:2–11).
- Peter and John saw a lame beggar on their path, and they healed him (Acts 3:1–10).
- Paul saw women by the river, and he taught them (Acts 16:13).

It is the compassion of Christ that will enable us to see past ourselves and find ways in which to love others. Scripture says, "When Jesus landed and saw a large crowd, he had compassion on them and healed their sick" (Matthew 14:14).

Some years ago, I was teaching the elders of one of our conferences about workplace evangelism, and in the evening we had time for some testimonies. One of the elders stood up and said, "I'm a very successful businessman—I own high-end car dealerships all over the state in which I live. But today for the first time I asked myself, 'What is the difference between me and any other successful businessman?' I want a fair profit, but so do they. I want to treat my employees well, but so do they. I want to deal with my customers with respect, but so do they. I want to get new customers, but so do they.

"Today I discovered that the difference is that I need to be concerned first and foremost about the eternal salvation of the people I deal with. I want God to change my perspective so that I'll think of these people as candidates for the kingdom of God rather than as just customers and employees. I need to pray for them, to minister to them, and to find creative ways to share Jesus with them. My preoccupation should be people and their salvation, not business or profit. I need to see these people as Jesus sees them—as His children. He died for them because He loves them so much."

Let your light shine

How do we shift our perception away from a preoccupation with self and worldly goods and toward the vision God has for humanity? The prophet Micah gives us this instruction, "He has told you, O man, what is good; and what does the LORD require of you but to do justice, to love kindness, and to walk humbly with your God?" (Micah 6:8, NASB).

When we have invested our lives in others—learning their hurts, mourning with them, feeling their inadequacies as our own—we are able to meet people where they are. Only when we've experienced the tug-of-war they face in life, only when we can call them by name and offer them comfort, is witnessing possible. As Christians, we are challenged to be different from those who live without Him. We are called to let our light shine before others (Matthew 5:16).

Ministry is not limited to those who get a paycheck for ministering. It is a divine command given to all believers—one that all of them are to live out.

Nothing we do will be of lasting effect unless it has been bathed in prayer and we have been empowered by the Holy Spirit. Without a deep sensitivity to the Spirit's leading, we cannot live before our neighbors and our fellow workers lives that reveal God and thus glorify Him. Our lifestyle should reveal our passion to reach people, our desire to do good to all people, and an appropriate awe and reverence for God. Investing in a day-to-day, long-term passion for developing a positive, Spirit-led, Christ-centered life will ultimately have the best impact in the sphere of our personal influence.

Section Three
Awe-Inspiring Worship

In this section we address ways in which you can make your worship services more transformative. This is done by making God the focus of every element in worship. The preliminaries, music, Scripture, and atmosphere are just as important as the sermon and must not be overlooked. So, your worship leaders must be trained.

Teach your congregation about worship and about the elements that make up the worship service. Help them understand why we do what we do each week. Make your worship services participatory—worship is not just sitting in a pew waiting to be fed by the sermon. And show your members that worship isn't reserved for the sanctuary of the church; it can be part of their daily lives.

Chapter 8
Twelve Ways to Improve
Your Worship Services

"Ascribe to the Lord, all you families of nations,
Ascribe to the Lord glory and strength.
Ascribe to the Lord the glory due his name;
Bring an offering and come before him.
Worship the Lord in the splendor of his holiness.
Tremble before him, all the earth!"—1 Chronicles 16:28–30

A church's worship services are meant to introduce people to God and to support the changes He makes in their lives. For more than three decades through both formal and informal means I have collected data in and about churches and their services. During that time I've also consulted with countless pastors, church-board members, worship leaders, and others. What I learned has made me believe that no matter how good a church's worship services are, it is likely that they can be improved. This chapter presents twelve things you can do to make your church's worship services more effective.

1. Form a worship committee

Having a worship committee will help your church develop and maintain engaging worship services.[1] Taking the time to train church members on how to plan and produce church services will not only free the pastor from that administrative task, but will also provide the members with a sense of involvement and ownership in the services.

The worship committee should find ways in which to make the worship service inclusive. It should get input from the congregation regarding preferences for music and worship styles. And it should set and maintain the local congregation's philosophy of worship.[2]

The worship committee can also work with the pastor to develop the preaching schedule for the year and to find topics that are relevant to both members and seekers. It can also help by finding videos and illustrations that will add variety to the services. And the committee can take the lead in planning special and seasonal programs for the church.[3]

2. Focus on God in every element of worship

The worship service should be a time dedicated to God. Evaluate your order of service and ask of every element, "Does this focus on God or the gospel?" If some of them don't, either remove them or push them to the beginning of the worship gathering. Specifically, such items as making announcements, greeting one another, and welcoming guests may have a legitimate place in the morning's program, but they should be handled in a way that won't break people's focus on the Lord.

It is the desire to worship God and to feel connected to Him that brings people to church each week. They long for closeness to God, which they may experience by gaining new insights that they will incorporate in their life or through what I call "God Moments." A God Moment is a time in the worship service when our hearts touch the heart of God and we have a vision of Him. It is making a connection with the Divine. Find a way in which your congregation can have a God Moment every week. Testimonies and prayer time can be just as effective as sermons when it comes to providing an opportunity to feel closer to God.

3. Don't allow the music to become a concert

Many people meet God in praise music. Increasingly, praise bands are singing songs that are inspirational, but that most of the congregation can't sing. They're popular tunes that are written for a talented lead vocalist, not for people whose range is a mere octave. So we in the pews are relegated to being spectators who watch the people on stage praise God.

Ellen White notes the need for using music in which all can participate. "In the meetings held, let a number be chosen to take part in the song service. And let the singing be accompanied with musical instruments skillfully handled. We are not to oppose the use of instruments of music in our work. This part of the service is to be carefully conducted; for it is the praise of God in song. *The singing is not always to be done by a few. As often as possible, let the entire congregation join.*"[4]

4. Don't interrupt the flow of worship

We've all been there. The music is awesome. Increasing numbers of the congregation are participating. Time is passing in a flash because they're meeting God through the experience. And the service comes to a crescendo with a prayer of thanksgiving that leaves some people wiping away tears. The Spirit has been ushered into this place in a mighty way. Then, abruptly, a worship leader asks the Spirit to sit quietly in a corner for ten minutes so we can take care of some housekeeping.

Sometimes this housekeeping is a set of announcements that people could just as easily read in the weekly bulletin. Sometimes it's a church member making a pitch for more participation in a budding ministry. Sometimes it's just taking time for the members to greet each other. Whatever the reason for the hiatus, it completely disrupts the God moment. People's hearts had been prepared to hear a powerful message from God's Word. Instead, they got the logistics for the church picnic.

Flow matters in a worship service, so make it a priority. Plan it. It's much better to go from singing directly into the sermon than to restrict the flow with intermissions that interrupt it.

Worship services should be uplifting and full of hope. A worship committee can work with the pastor to make sure that the service is not made up of unconnected bits and pieces. Have each element of the service coordinate with the theme of the day. Ideally, the congregational singing, prayer time, children's story, Scripture readings, and special music should all point to the message of the sermon. Having the message presented in various ways will benefit all those present and reach those of all learning styles.

> **The Composition of the Worship Committee**
>
> Typically, the worship committee is comprised of
>
> - the worship coordinator
> - the music director
> - the choir director
> - the children's ministry/drama coordinator
> - the audio visual director
> - select elders
> - creative laypeople
> - a member of the pastoral staff
>
> Note that in small churches, many of these positions overlap and/or don't exist at all.

5. Allow guests to remain anonymous

Research shows that most people visiting a church for the first time want to remain anonymous.[5] If they don't, they'll introduce themselves after the service. The *last* thing newcomers want is to "stand up so we can show you how much we appreciate you." Most long-time members don't want to be singled out and brought to everyone's attention—how much less must a first-time guest desire this!

One church I attended sought to mitigate what they considered to be a problem by asking first-time guests to remain seated while everyone else stood to greet them. Since *standing out* is the problem, this creative tactic didn't help much. Worship leaders might do well to become a first-time guest for a week

Important Things to Consider

- Start on time. If you don't, guests who have arrived on time may be tempted to leave rather than wait. And when you start late, you'll end late, and hungry adults and children will start squirming and destroy the spiritual atmosphere.
- Make every worship service a positive experience. People should feel hopeful and inspired when they leave.
- Build variety into your worship services to keep them interesting. Don't be afraid to add drama and/or videos or to change the style of music.
- Educate your congregation as to how and why we worship.
- Keep the children's story to approximately five minutes in length. Make sure the presenter has enthusiasm and can relate to kids.
- Determine what length of service fits your congregation best and plan accordingly. If your service is longer than the locals think it should be, they'll leave before you're done and they won't return.
- Ask often for feedback—this will help you determine which parts of the service are beneficial and which need improvement.
- Strive to appeal to both the emotions (through music and stories) and the mind (through sound exegesis and biblical exposition).
- Worship leaders "should devote some time to practice, that they may employ this talent to the glory of God."* Practice every part of the worship service, not just the music. It is by mindful practice that we hone our God-given talents so we can give glory to Him.
- In every worship service, contemplate the Word of God, celebrate the gospel, and rejoice in the change God makes in the believer.

---

* Ellen G. White, *The Voice in Speech and Song* (Nampa, Idaho: Pacific Press®, 1988), 434.

in a church where they don't know anyone, and no one there knows them. This would remind them how uncomfortable one feels at being singled out.

Seeker-friendly churches realize that there are better times to greet guests than when all eyes are on them. They try to avoid singling people out with an impersonal mass greeting. Instead, they take the time to start conversations and get to know newcomers on an individual level. Welcome centers and fellowship meals after the worship service are good ways to connect with guests.

6. Eliminate prayers that really are speeches

When Jesus taught us how we should pray, He provided as a model a prayer that goes from zero to done in under thirty seconds. By contrast, many of our pulpit prayers are five to ten minutes long. Jesus said, "When you pray, do not keep on babbling like pagans, for they think they will be heard because of their many words" (Matthew 6:7).

Talking to God is a good thing—we all need to do more of it. But Ellen White advises that while our private prayers may be long ones, we should keep our public prayers short, and we should avoid preaching during our prayers—that is the role of the sermon.[6] In our worship services, let the worship leader pray briefly and earnestly and then allow the worshipers to pray or meditate in silence for a time.

7. Delegate so you'll have the time you need for sermon preparation

Many pastors are overwhelmed with administrative demands that take time away from sermon preparation. Consequently, they're left to squeeze in what time they can for preparation—sometimes at the expense of their families and their health. After they deliver the message, those in the pews smile, nod, and thank them for the sermon. But the congregation could have learned a whole lot more from what the speaker said, and could have had a better worship experience, had the pastor been given more time to invest in that message.

Preachers who want to teach with excellence need adequate time to prepare. Effective pastors of growing churches spend between twelve and twenty hours a week preparing their sermons.[7] They need time to research their topic, put it in an engaging format, make sure the points flow, and practice their delivery. Even more basic than that, any Christian who desires to teach well needs the time and resources for spiritual and professional development. When we stop learning, our teaching suffers immeasurably.

Those who want to deliver life-changing messages week after week may need to change the work system in their churches. They must be able to off-load many of their administrative tasks, giving them to well-trained church members so they can focus on teaching with excellence.[8]

8. Teach people how Scripture applies to daily living

After a seminar I conducted on transformational Bible reading, a number of pastors told me that they had never heard the Bible used in such a way. One man said, "You speak of practical things using spiritual language." To these people, the Bible was about theology or eschatology but had little to say regarding day-to-day living.

This problem occurs around the world each weekend as pastors neglect the highly practical nature of God's Word. When was the last time you heard a solid sermon about how to live your faith in the workplace? Or about biblical principles for raising your kids? Or about how to resolve conflicts in a biblically consistent manner? Or about how to witness in your daily life? Or about how to be a positive influence in your community? The Bible speaks to all these areas, but many Christians don't know it.

Great pulpit messages are great, in part, because they show how to apply scriptural lessons to daily life. We are "to preach for transformation—and that is done by application teaching."[9] People are starving for more than just good advice. A study of the New Testament letter writers and great preachers throughout history show that their epistles and sermons were at least 50 percent application.[10] If we begin to take practical theology seriously, we'll be amazed how many people in the pews will begin to take serious notes.

9. Don't give destinations without giving directions

Pastors are remarkably good at identifying targets. Love God with all your heart. Listen for God's voice. Demonstrate joy, peace, kindness, and so on. Live out the Great Commission. Turn the other cheek. Love your neighbor as yourself.

We should co-labor with God to pursue such ideals. However, I've left countless services wondering just *how* I can make progress. What am I supposed to do? I've learned about the desirability of the destination, but I've been disheartened because I've not been told how to get to that wonderful state.

When pastors teach that we should be more patient, they should also teach *how* to become more patient. When encouraging believers to evangelize, they should share what works in persuading people to consider the claims of the gospel. Preachers should show their congregations how to live the Christian life with joy and effectiveness.

The best teachers and preachers recognize this issue and therefore seldom offer applications without a "how." They are highly practical in their teaching. As a result, their members walk out of each service with an action plan to make real progress that week and beyond.

This is no small issue. Preachers who give their congregations destinations without directions, who now know how far they have to go without knowing how to get there, frustrate their congregations. Just as we'd carefully spell out directions from point A to point Z for a lost traveler, we should provide clear road maps for the many travelers making a stop in our pews.

10. Shorten the sermon—and focus it

Want to know the fastest way to depress a pastor? Have him or her ask people on Sabbath evening what points were made that morning. If you want to totally demoralize him or her, ask the question on Tuesday. I recently asked a group of friends on Saturday night what they remembered. Only 20 percent of them could answer correctly. And on Tuesday, only one person could articulate what the sermon had been about.

The sad reality is that in an era of information overload, we no longer remember the vast majority of what we hear. We might remember one of the jokes or stories from the presentation, but the essential lessons are gone.

You can help your listeners to remember the message by shortening the sermon.[11] I read aloud and slowly Jesus' most substantial sermon, the Sermon on the Mount. I got through the whole thing in less than twelve minutes!

"I'll have to cut out so much!" some will object. From a teaching perspective that's a good thing! Rather than presenting three points or steps, focus on one main point, one "homiletical bullet."[12] Andy Stanley warns, "If you give people too much to remember, they won't remember anything. . . . Everything you say can be life-changing, but if they can't remember it then it won't change a thing. . . . You've got to narrow the focus of your message to one point. Then everything else in the message supports, illustrates, and helps make it memorable."[13] Show it visually. Use humor and emotion to make the point. And especially, tell stories that illustrate it. That was Jesus' approach to teaching—He told stories because people remember stories. I cannot remember the book of Amos, but I remember very well the book of Jonah because it is a story.

I try to remember the advice of my wife: always leave them wanting more.

11. Challenge people

Pastors may not be willing to require much of their hearers because they are afraid that if they present God as desiring them to act out their beliefs, people will reject their teaching. So, they preach a low-cost Christianity. Challenge people to change. Challenge them individually and collectively to be examples of the transformational power of Christ. Challenge them to be introspective, to see themselves against the blazing benchmark of Scripture, to become more sanctified, and to go out and change their little corner of the world for God's kingdom. This can be done without the use of guilt or manipulation. Show people that they're on an adventure with God—an adventure that requires both courage and commitment.

That's what Jesus did. He told people to let their light shine, to go and sin no more. He told them to take up the cross and follow Him.

The call of God is both exciting and exacting. Churches that boldly speak the truth in love are growing, but more important, they're growing real disciples.

12. Pray for the presence of the Holy Spirit

Ultimately, it's not the form of the service conducted, the talents of the worship leaders, or the persuasiveness of the sermons that determines the effectiveness of the worship service. It's the conviction of the Holy Spirit that brings these results. It is the power of the Spirit that convicts hearts and changes lives. The churches where God is worshiped and glorified and where people are changed and transformed are churches that pray a lot. They pray before, during, and after the worship service. In many of them, members take the time to go into the sanctuary and pray over all of the pews for everyone who is coming to church and ask God to show up and do something amazing in their midst. If you want to improve your worship service, pray a lot.

If anything is worth doing well, it is the worship of our glorious God. We shouldn't expect to see changes in worship without prayer and the work of the Holy Spirit, but neither should we expect to see our worship enhanced without taking initiative. It is by intentional planning, practice, and communication that we will be able to provide a worship service that honors God while edifying and uplifting members and guests.

---

1. I have used the information I present in this chapter when forming my own worship committee and when advising others who have asked about forming worship committees in their churches. The feedback I received from those churches has been very positive; they felt that the worship committee added structure, depth, variety, and inspiration to their worship services.

2. Rich DuBose, "Should Your Church Have a Worship Committee?" Advent Source, accessed July 23, 2015, http://www.adventsource.org/as30/plusLine.article.aspx?id=208&umschk=1.

3. For those pastoring more than one church, a worship committee will help add continuity and save time for the pastor since committee members are responsible for planning the weekly services. See Sidebar 2 for a list of who should be on a worship committee.

4. Ellen G. White, *Gospel Workers* (Washington, D.C.: Review and Herald®, 1915), 357, 358; emphasis added.

5. For those who have left the church and are returning, only 11 percent want to identify themselves as a visitor per a LifeWay study ("Formerly Churched Prefer to Remain Anonymous," LifeWay Research, November 6, 2006, accessed July 22, 2015, http://www.lifewayresearch .com/2006/11/06/formerly-churched-prefer-to-remain-anonymous/), and according to Barna, only 22 percent of visitors like being asked to identify themselves (George Barna, *Evangelism That Works* [Ventura, Calif.: Regal Books, 1995], 67.)

6. "But many offer prayer in a dry, sermonizing manner. These pray to men, not to God. . . . They are made no account of in heaven. Angels of God are wearied with them, as well as mortals who are compelled to listen to them." Ellen G. White, *Testimonies for the Church*, 2:581, 582.

7. Thom S. Rainer, *Surprising Insights From the Unchurched and Proven Ways to Reach Them* (Grand Rapids, Mich.: Zondervan, 2008), 209–222. A more recent survey by Thom Rainer noted that 70 percent of pastors spend ten to eighteen hours of preparation on each sermon. See Thom S. Rainer, "How Much Time Do Pastors Spend Preparing a Sermon?" Thom S. Rainer (blog), accessed July 21, 2015, http://thomrainer.com/2013/06/how-much-time-do-pastors-spend -preparing-a-sermon/. Pastors working with a smaller church or a multichurch district may not be able to put in as much sermon prep time due to a lack of administrative help. (See the example of Tim Keller in Eric McKiddie, "Should You Take 2 Hours or 32 Hours for Sermon Prep?" Sermon Central, accessed July 21, 2015, http://www.sermoncentral.com/pastors-preaching -articles/eric-mckiddie-should-you-take-2-hours-or-32-hours-for-sermon-prep-1730.asp.) However, in a multichurch district pastors usually will be preaching the same sermon, adjusted for context, at each of the different churches, and therefore during some weeks they will have extra time for training or preparing for sermons to be preached sometime in the future.

8. The quality of the sermon is often a major factor when people are deciding to return to a

church. Roger Walter, "A Collaborative Sermon Preparation Team at the Seventh-day Adventist Community Church of Vancouver, WA" (DMin diss., Andrews University Seventh-day Adventist Theological Seminary, 2012), 3.

9. Rick Long, "Preaching for Life Change," Church Leaders, accessed July 23, 2015 http:// www.churchleaders.com/pastors/preaching-teaching/138265-rick-long-preaching-for-life -change.html.

10. Michael Duduit, "Purpose-Driven Preaching: An Interview With Rick Warren," Preaching .com, September 1, 2001, accessed July 23, 2015, http://www.preaching.com/resources /articles/11565775/.

11. I do acknowledge that the generational and cultural makeup of the congregation will have an impact on the sermon length they prefer. Surveys tend to have mixed results when people are asked if sermons should be longer or shorter per Thom S. Rainer, "Three Views on How Long a Sermon Should Be," accessed July 28, 2015, http://thomrainer.com/2014/07/three-views-long -sermon/. The quality of the content also carries weight. A short sermon that is well researched and delivered can have more impact than one that goes on tangents to fill the time. Likewise, a long sermon with substance will be more beneficial to the congregation than a short sermon that is full of fluff. See Chris Thompson, "Chris Thompson: Does the length of the sermon matter?" *Alaska Dispatch News,* July 12, 2014, accessed July 28, 2015, http://www.adn.com /article/20140712/chris-thompson-does-length-sermon-matter.

12. Derek J. Morris and Haddon W. Robinson, "Bullets or Buckshot?" *Ministry* 73, no. 9 (September 2000): 22–25. Also see Terry G. Carter, J. Scott Duvall, and J. Daniel Hays, *Preaching God's Word: A Hands-On Approach to Preparing, Developing, and Delivering the Sermon* (Grand Rapids, Mich.: Zondervan, 2005), 101.

13. Andy Stanley and Lane Jones, *Communicating for a Change: Seven Keys to Irresistible Communication*, North Point Resources Series (Portland, Ore.: Multnomah Books, 2006), 39–41.

Chapter 9
Worship Education

"Come, let us sing for joy to the LORD*; let us shout aloud to the Rock of our*
salvation.
Let us come before him with thanksgiving and extol him with music and song.
For the LORD *is the great God, the great King above all gods.*
In his hand are the depths of the earth, and the mountain peaks belong to him.
The sea is his, for he made it, and his hands formed the dry land.
Come, let us bow down in worship, let us kneel before the LORD *our Maker;*
for he is our God and we are the people of his pasture, the flock under his
care."—Psalm 95:1–7

Most Christians would say that corporate worship is critically important. Yet, in church after church, the worship service is woefully underdeveloped. Often, this centerpiece of the Christian community is dull and lifeless. As a result, worshipers check out. They either leave the service mentally, daydreaming to pass the time, or look for a church where they feel that God is present.

It doesn't have to be this way in any Christian church. Every local congregation can have inspiring worship services if the leaders are willing to make serious investments in worship. Obviously this means praying, planning, and finding talents and resources. In addition, education and training are important both for worship leaders and for the congregation. "Unless correct ideas of true worship and true reverence are impressed upon the people, there will be a growing tendency to place the sacred and eternal on a level with common things, and those professing the truth will be an offense to God and a disgrace to religion."[1]

We must not assume that people become knowledgeable in worship simply by attending church services. Leaders should develop a plan for teaching believers to be genuine worshipers.

Worship concepts

There are several key aspects of corporate worship that worship leaders would do well to teach their congregations:

1. The priority of worship. Our highest calling is to glorify God, so the church must give this top priority. Worship is serious business that deserves a congregation's greatest investment. It isn't to be contained within the walls of the church nor within the hour or so of Sabbath morning services. Worship should be a weeklong process that climaxes during the corporate church service.

The psalms are full of praise and worship directed to the awesome God who is not only Creator but also Savior and King. Being in the presence of the Lord should be a humbling experience. According to Peter, David made his life one of worship. He repeats what David said about the Creator/Savior/King:

> "I saw the Lord always before me.
>   Because he is at my right hand,
>   I will not be shaken.
> Therefore my heart is glad and my tongue rejoices;
>   my body also will rest in hope"
>   (Acts 2:25, 26).

David didn't limit worship to the sanctuary service. He was always in the presence of God, and that filled him with joy, stability, and hope.

2. The purpose of worship. Worship is primarily an activity in which the worshipers declare the attributes and glory of God. As worshipers learn to magnify His name and declare His mighty deeds through songs, reading of the Bible, testimonies, exhortation, and worship, they are ushered into the inspiring presence of God.

Worship isn't just a simple proclamation of the greatness of God. It penetrates the worshipers, transforming them. "Worship is the submission of all our nature to God. It is the quickening of conscience by His holiness; the nourishment of mind with His truth; the purifying of imagination by His Beauty; the opening of the heart to His love; the surrender of will to His purpose—and all of this gathered up in adoration, the most selfless emotion of which our nature is capable and therefore the chief remedy for that self-centeredness which is our original sin and the source of all actual sin."[2]

3. The principles of worship. I have discovered that teaching people the following principles increases their understanding of worship, which increases their participation. Worship should

- glorify God through encouraging worshipers to make a radical commitment to Him;
- focus upon Jesus Christ by making Him the center of every part of the worship service;
- edify believers through fellowship, encouragement, service, ministry, and prayer; and

- appeal to visitors by being seeker-friendly in what you say and what you do.

While most congregations follow some of the above principles of worship, they all should be evident—including that of service. The idea that service should be part of worship may be new to some. However, Ellen White has noted, "True worship consists in working together with Christ. Prayers, exhortation, and talk are cheap fruits, which are frequently tied on; but fruits that are manifested in good works, in caring for the needy, the fatherless, and widows, are genuine fruits, and grow naturally upon a good tree."[3]

Jesus also noted that our involvement in service should play a role in our worship. He said, "Worship the Lord your God, and serve[4] him only" (Matthew 4:10). Believers should seek ways in which they can serve others throughout the week. The church encourages this by providing regular opportunities to serve in the church or in the community—for example, painting a member's house, fixing a car, or mowing the lawn of someone who's incapacitated.

4. The practices of worship. Worship leaders may wrongly assume that believers understand the forms of worship simply because they see them as they participate in the worship service. By educating worshipers regarding the background, meaning, and purpose of these worship forms, leaders equip men and women to engage wholeheartedly in the activities of praise and worship.

Corporate worship often takes on the attributes of those participating in it. Since each person attending the worship service influences its "shape" and influence, we must be aware of what we are projecting to those in our congregations. Do we genuinely enjoy joining with our fellow members in praising God, or do we attend the weekly worship services because we're expected to do that? The Bible recounts many examples of joyful worship: 1 Chronicles 15:16 tells us of David's request to have Levites appointed "as musicians to make a joyful sound"; Psalm 100 portrays people praising God; and Revelation 19 depicts heavenly rejoicing and people shouting their praise. Scripture instructs us to "continually offer to God a sacrifice of praise" (Hebrews 13:16). And Ellen White tells us that "the lifeless attitude of the worshipers in the house of God is one great reason why the ministry is not more productive of good. The melody of song, poured forth from many hearts in clear, distinct utterance, is one of God's instrumentalities in the work of saving souls. All the service should be conducted with solemnity and awe, as if in the visible presence of the Master of assemblies."[5]

5. The power of worship. Worship may be engaging even without God's presence, but when He's not there, it isn't life-transforming. Only the Spirit of God can heal the broken and redeem the lost. He must be the congregation's most welcomed and honored guest. So, the worship leaders should instruct the worshipers to pray that the Holy Spirit will fill us.

It was worship that moved Isaiah to action. He saw the glory of God and felt the weight of his sinful nature. Because of this he was able to experience the gospel. This intimate worship encounter filled Isaiah with gratitude and inspired Him to accept God's call to service (Isaiah 6:1–8).

Worship instruction

As part of my doctoral work, I studied what effect worship education had on the worship experience of the congregation. At my church, which, at the time, had an average attendance of 290 people, we spent eight weeks focusing on why we worship and what the elements of worship mean. Before we started this intentional worship education, 39 percent of the people surveyed felt that participation during the service ("God speaks and I respond") was important, but by the end of the eight weeks, 58 percent of all those surveyed and 63 percent of those who had attended all eight weeks recognized the importance of participation. I was encouraged when I learned that all the worship practices became more meaningful to the congregation when their understanding of worship increased. This includes praise, fellowship with other believers, sermons, Bible studies, corporate prayers, and offerings. There was also an increase of almost 15 percent in the number of people who now felt the importance of regular church attendance.[6] I found that education not only increased knowledge but also intensified individual experience in worship.

Pastors and worship leaders should make maximum use of a variety of media and formats for instructing believers regarding worship concepts. There are at least five specific things worship leaders can do to increase the congregation's understanding of the elements of worship.

1. Prepare a "Philosophy of Ministry and Worship" document. Every church should develop and distribute a philosophy of ministry and worship document. This will include the style of worship for each service. For example, one church may want a blended or traditional service in order to connect with the past and with the older members, while another church—one that prioritizes reaching the youth and new believers—might choose a more contemporary worship style. This document will serve as a guide to establishing the theological priorities of the congregation. The five elements of worship (prayer, Word, fellowship, offering, and ministry) should be included, providing a beginning knowledge base for further worship training.

2. Develop a visitor's guide to worship. Most visitors approach the worship service with a certain degree of anxiety born out of the unknown. As much as possible, help visitors feel at ease by developing a guide that clearly defines the purpose and practice of worship at your church. When the worship leaders increase people's understanding, they also increase their participation.

3. In the classes held for potential and new members, discuss the various issues related to worship. Membership classes are very important to the health of a congregation—every church should have an ongoing membership class. These classes should provide seminars on the church's—the denomination's—doctrines and history; the history, mission, and vision of the local church; spiritual gifts; and worship philosophy. This will enable newcomers to learn, understand, and embrace the priorities of the body before they make their membership commitment. If worship is in fact top priority, be sure to address it during at least one session of the membership instruction series. Here are some suggestions on what to cover:

- What worship is
- What corporate worship is
- How to behave in a way that encourages worship
- What to expect from the worship service
  - Feeling God's presence
  - Experiencing God's grace
  - Feeling loved by the community of faith
  - Allowing the Holy Spirit to change you
  - Being led and motivated to serve others
  - Concluding with hope because God is in control
- What the church expects from worship
  - An open heart and positive attitude
  - A praying spirit
  - Participation and engagement (singing, offerings, fellowship, exhortation, prayer, service, attentiveness)

I recommend that these classes be conducted every three to four months. They usually take place over the course of two Sabbaths; expect to spend three hours each Sabbath afternoon eating a meal and going over the information. Having a philosophy of ministry document and a visitor's guide will help you with these classes.

4. Instruct worshipers during the weekly worship service. One of the churches that I pastored focused on instructing the congregants as the worship service proceeded. Every week we creatively explained to them the elements of the worship service that they were experiencing. We also highlighted particular worship practices that we thought people might misunderstand, such as why offering is a part of worship. Here again, education leads to new understanding and increased participation.

5. Develop a series of sermons on the subject of worship. Every pastor who preaches on the topic of worship has a great opportunity to initiate change.

Pastors would do well to develop one or more topical sermons on each of the five concepts and elements of worship. Because your congregation is shifting from—and being tempted to fall back on—what had been their worship practices, consider doing a sermon series on worship once every three years. Possible sermon topics could be "What Is Worship?"; "Praise and Worship"; "Offering and Worship"; "The Thrill of Worship"; "Witnessing and Worship"; and "Prayer and Worship."

No responsible corporation would encourage its employees to do their jobs without proper training, and the more critical the area of responsibility, the more vital the preparation is. *Worship is the single most important event in the life of the Christian, for everything in Christianity centers on worship.* The health and vitality of the believers rise and fall based on the vigor of their worship experience. Worship is the commemoration of Creation and the celebration of the gospel. It is the believer's response to the mercy and goodness of God through adoration, reverence, thanksgiving, obedience, and submission. Christians worship because of what God has done, is doing, and will do through His Son Jesus Christ and through His Spirit. Of all the activities of the local church, worship must have *top priority*!

---

1. White, *Testimonies for the Church*, 5:500.

2. William Temple, *Readings in St. John's Gospel*, quoted in Bob Kauflin, "Defining Worship, Part 1," Worship Matters, November 4, 2005, http://www.worshipmatters.com/2005/11/04 /defining-worship/.

3. Ellen G. White, *Christian Service* (Washington, D.C.: Review and Herald®, 1947), 96.

4. It is interesting to note that the word used here as meaning *serve* can also be translated as *worship*. See Bible Hub, s.v. "3000. latreuó," http://biblehub.com/greek/3000.htm.

5. White, *Testimonies for the Church*, 5:493.

6. S. Joseph Kidder, "Education for Worship in the East Wenatchee Seventh-day Adventist Church" (DMin diss., Andrews University, 1996), 119.

Section Four
Engaging and Transformational Preaching

Sermons usually take up a large part of the worship service, and the congregation expects to be taught and inspired by what is presented from the pulpit. Consequently, then, pastors and the other worship leaders should prepare their sermons well.

This section of this book has three chapters. I've split the topic The Top Twenty Ways to Improve Your Sermon into two chapters—one on preparation for writing a sermon and the other on content essential to the actual writing of the sermon. By continually increasing your knowledge base and skill set, you will grow in your ability to minister to your congregation. These tips will also be helpful for those who teach Sabbath School classes or tell the children's story. In fact, everyone who has a role in the worship service will find helpful material in this section.

In this section I also propose that you consider using the sermonic year system. That means planning your sermon topics and worship services a year at a time. When you do so, you can work with your church leaders and be intentional about the themes and messages you wish to present to your congregation. This approach makes it easy for you to balance nurturing, evangelism, and assimilation. You can also plan how you will approach the seasons—such as Thanksgiving and Christmas—and how best to address community needs and highlight evangelistic series. While planning a sermonic year involves a lot of work, the benefits are abundant.

Chapter 10
The Top Twenty Ways to Improve
Your Preaching—Part 1

"How beautiful on the mountains are the feet of those who bring good news, who proclaim peace, who bring good tidings, who proclaim salvation, who say to Zion, 'Your God reigns!' "—Isaiah 52:7

"Preach the word; be prepared in season and out of season; correct, rebuke and encourage—with great patience and careful instruction."—2 Timothy 4:2

I know I'm not the best preacher on the planet—but I wish I were. While every believer has the privilege of sharing the good news of the Prince of Peace, preachers have the blessing of making it their lifework. That's why I'm passionate about improving.

This chapter and the next comprise a list of suggestions you can use to become a more effective preacher or teacher. They're collections of some things I've learned along the way—some of which I am currently trying to implement in my preaching and teaching. This first chapter deals with practical preparation elements while the next chapter will address elements, related to the content of your sermons. Here are my top twenty things you can do to improve your preaching.

20. Grow in your knowledge and experience

No matter how well you preach, eventually you're going to become predictable. We're very familiar with the way things work for us—so familiar, perhaps, that we lose that fresh sense of wonder that used to come as we prepared to preach. Yet freshness is essential to good preaching. An infusion of fresh subjects and fresh modes of delivering them is beneficial lest we become predictable and routine. Here are some things you can do to overcome the problem of staleness.

- Read a lot—especially from the Bible. Daily contact with the Word of

God will refresh your life, so continue to read and reread the Bible. Also, read books on spiritual growth, Christian values, and doctrine. Read commentaries and reference books. Read books on preaching, biographies, the newspaper, and anything else that might help you become a better preacher. Even with a heavy preaching and teaching schedule, I make time to read at least two books every month.

- Once or twice a year attend a class or seminar on some issue. You can find seminars available on topics such as culture and trends and preaching. Keep an eye out for free seminars, which often are offered at local colleges or libraries.

Subscribe to a good sermon service. Most of us want to write our own sermons. I know I do. Realistically, though, there are times when I need help—or at least I need a good idea or a fresh perspective. The typical preacher goes through about forty sermons a year.

A good sermon service, such as the Preaching Today Web site, can help you stay ahead of the curve. Of course, you won't rely on this service for all your sermons any more than you would use your commentaries or books in that way. Find what's best for you and your listeners—the things that are biblically sound. Weigh them carefully, correct them where needed, and filter them through your own way of communicating. For a relatively small cost, you won't be caught again without good ideas and resources.

When I suggest to my students the importance of growth through reading, seminars, classes, and various services of preaching, they protest, "That will cost too much money and take too much time." I tell them, "Spending money to grow or to become more effective—to be the best you can be—honors God!"

19. Listen to and read great sermons

When you hear or read someone else's sermon, look for the best that he or she has to offer. Iron sharpens iron, and listening to good preaching will sharpen you. You can find sermons on the radio, on CDs, and on the Web. If you hear a good sermon, take it apart and examine the structure. If it's really good, transcribe it and analyze it. You'll benefit from the effort.

18. Start a filing system that works for you and stick with it

Preachers need to be able to store good material in a way that allows them to find it when they need it. I've tried a number of systems over the years and have settled on one that allows me to painlessly catalog the stories and other materials that I want to keep in both electronic and paper forms and to do so without hiring a full-time librarian.

My system is very simple. I put one of three letters—A, B, or S—on everything I file. If I read something that I really like and that I know will take less than ten hours to turn into a sermon, I mark it with the letter A. If what I have is a seed to be used in the future and I estimate that it will take more than ten hours to develop into a sermon, I mark it with a B. And if what I have won't make a sermon but will work as an illustration or introduction, I mark it with the letter S.

Then I file it under the heading that fits it best, but I also put references to it in folders on other topics that it also fits, indicating the folder in which I've filed the story. The key point is to file whatever you have under multiple topics so you can find it easily. For instance, I might file a story I've found under such categories as hope, faith, and the Second Coming. Then, when I need a story for a sermon on one of these topics, I can find this one.

17. Make collecting illustrations your passion

Illustrations often make the difference between good preaching and great preaching. Having just the right story or analogy at just the right time will do wonders for you and your listeners. Let me heartily recommend *Parson's Bible Illustrator* (the deluxe version) as the greatest single aid you can find in this area. It is reasonably priced, and if I lost the one I have, I would make acquiring another one my first order of business.

16. Improve your storytelling technique

Telling a story is more effective than reading one. We all love to hear a story told well. When you intend to relate an incident or anecdote or to repeat a Bible story, give special attention to your presentation. Here's your opportunity to add vocal color to what might otherwise be a black-and-white speech.

In effect, you are a professional storyteller. Make the telling of your story—even a Bible story that your congregation has heard hundreds of times—a thing of beauty. If you can, attend a storytelling convention and observe how the masters work. Here are a few tips of theirs that you can borrow.

- Visualize the characters and setting so fully that your listeners can see in their mind's eye what you are seeing. Allow them to put themselves in the story.
- Don't be afraid to move and gesture.
- Use your voice the way an actor would. Change voice characterizations as you convey the words of the different speakers in your story. Vary the speed, tone, and volume you use.

Listen to and watch other preachers and public speakers. Don't copy them—when you preach, you should sound like yourself. But learn from the good preachers and public speakers you run across.

15. Carry an iPod or notebook and use a diary

I nearly always have an iPod or a small notebook with me. If I'm in the car between appointments and I hear something good on the radio, out comes the iPod, and I get it down before I forget it. If a good idea pops up in my mind, the iPod is out again and I dictate the thought before it escapes. I take this little device with me every morning when I walk, and it goes with me nearly everywhere else too. I even take it on vacation. Good ideas have a way of disappearing if we don't catch them.

Recently, I've begun using a computer diary, and I've found that if I transfer the random things I've collected from the iPod to the diary at the end of each day, I can take full advantage of them later. I use a shareware program called My Personal Diary.

14. Mentor someone or find someone to mentor you

Many of those who write to me say that though they learned much in seminary, they learn even more when someone personally tutors them. Young preachers can benefit from observing older, "seasoned" preachers, and those "seasoned" preachers can find new energy and challenge in mentoring someone younger. When I graduated from the seminary and started pastoring, I asked my ministerial director to point out for me the best pastors in my conference. I wanted to have them mentor me in various areas. That was one of the most helpful things I did. I learned a lot about preaching, church growth, and conflict management from those pastors. I also got into a mentoring program with three of my friends. We shared books, listened to each other preach, and got helpful comments.

Choose your mentor carefully. When you find one, treat him or her with honor and respect.

13. Be your own toughest critic

Watch for ways to improve your presentations. Trying something new may make you feel self-conscious at first, but the benefits are worth it. You would be wise to assume that you'll need to make improvements. It's easy to get into a rut. Over the years you may have developed an annoying habit or two, or at least lost some of the enthusiasm and charm that came more naturally in the earlier years of your ministry. It takes courage to ask people to give you objective, constructive criticism, but it might be worth it—especially if it's been years since your classmates in Homiletics 501 pointed out your flaws.

In addition to getting someone else's critique, you can evaluate and upgrade your speaking ability yourself. Don't be fooled. Listen, and ask yourself the following:

- Would you listen to what you're saying if you didn't have to?
- Can you summarize what you said in three sentences or less? In other words, did you have a clearly identifiable theme?
- Are you having trouble concentrating on what you said?
- Does the audience react to your voice? Do they laugh in the right places, or are they coughing and squirming, which indicates that you've lost them?
- Can most twelve-year-olds understand the words you use? Can they grasp the content of your sermons?
- What do you want people to do when they've heard your sermon? Is there an action point? If you can't answer that question, then you haven't completed your sermon. If you don't find your sermon to be meaningful and transformational, then pray some more and study some more.

Ask people for honest feedback, and don't let them off the hook until they tell you something you can do better. It is this honest, sometimes harsh, but constructive criticism that has been the most helpful to me.

People tend to remember carefully constructed principles or powerful stories. Make sure your message has one or the other, if not both. Remember, our opinions don't matter as much as we think they do. Preach the Word of God, not your personal preferences or ideas.

12. Ask God to make you into a better servant

"Unless the Lord builds the house, they labor in vain who build it" (Psalm 127:1, NASB). Prayer, discipline, integrity, honesty, humility, and the reminder of whom you are working for are critical to good preaching. Allow God to work on you as you work on the message.

Remember that your sermons should be about God first and people second. And don't preach about yourself. To test whether you have avoided this trap, count how many times you say "I" and "me" in your sermons.

Now that we have discussed the importance of adequate preparation, turn the page for some tips on how to improve the content of your sermons.

Chapter 11
The Top Twenty Ways to Improve
Your Preaching—Part 2

"This is eternal life: that they know you, the only true God, and Jesus Christ, whom you have sent."—John 17:3

In the previous chapter we looked at some great tips on how to prepare to write a sermon. In this chapter, I present some things to keep in mind regarding the content of your sermons.

11. Keep Jesus at the center

Every sermon should be about Jesus. "Theoretical discourses are essential, that people may see the chain of truth, link after link, uniting in a perfect whole; but no discourse should ever be preached without presenting Christ and Him crucified as the foundation of the gospel. Ministers would reach more hearts if they would dwell more upon practical godliness."[1]

If your sermon is not about Jesus, then keep working on it or start over. No matter what you are preaching about, include a gospel presentation. Jesus said, "If I be lifted up I will draw all men unto me" (see John 12:32).

10. Build tension

Since you are preaching with a purpose, there will be some kind of opposition. Here's a truth right out of Matthew 5: "Love your enemies" (verse 44). Yes, you must tell people that they need to do this and why they need to do it. But don't stop there. Tell them as well what challenges they'll face if they try to obey this command of Jesus. Expose the objections and mind-sets that get in the way. Show that a love for self and material things will always suffocate a love for God and other people. Tease the truth out and put it on display. A good question to ask is "What are the obstacles to obeying this truth?"

You can also acknowledge the tension raised by trying to put into practice the truth that you are presenting. For example, we are called to forgive each other. Well, what about those who won't repent or confess? How do we handle that? And how does seventy times seven play out? Bring to the forefront the questions that the truth you are preaching raises. Your people are already thinking it, so go ahead and work it out.

9. Use word pictures

Do you want to liven up your sermons? Hang some pictures on the walls. Paint some rooms. Open some windows. Sermons shouldn't smell as if they've been in a musty old closet. You need to put some air, some life, and some color in them.

This whole world is stamped with God's creative seal, so find something there that illustrates, elucidates, or communicates your point and go get it. If you want more help understanding how to do this, read Jesus' Sermon on the Mount or Paul's epistles. Metaphors abound. Believers are compared to salt, light, and the human body, and spirituality is pictured as a set of armor and an Olympic race. Help your congregation to see for themselves the glories of God's Word. Fill your sermon with word pictures. Mark Twain once said, "The difference between the right word and the almost right word is the difference between lightning and the lightning bug." Strive to use the right words. This will make a great difference in your preaching.

8. Be interesting

It takes work to convey the same message (of love) fifty-two weeks a year without repeating yourself or using worn-out phrases, clichés, professional jargon, or pat answers. If you're playing the same record Sabbath after Sabbath, look around for a fresh slant, a new angle, or an unusual viewpoint. Here are some ways to be more interesting:

- Spend more time preparing your sermons—fifteen to twenty hours.
- Leave out the boring bits. The more focused the sermon, the better off you are.
- Preach your sermon to people whom you know will be honest in their critique.
- Ditch your notes. Memorizing your sermon allows you to be audience-driven rather than notes-driven.
- Speak to the people who aren't there yet. Be evangelistic in nature.
- Speak to the people who are there. Be nurturing.
- Talk about and lift up Jesus every week.
- Include a great story. The best stories are personal ones.
- Tell your members how to act on what they've heard.
- Pray as if your life depends on it. The greatest task in preaching is not

the preparation of the sermon but the preparation of the heart. Let God speak to you and fill you with His grace and love.

7. Be creative

Being creative doesn't mean that you have to become an entertainer or even change your preaching style significantly. There are three main ways in which to use creativity to bring life into your sermons. First, draw new insights from a very familiar story. Research the cultural significance of the elements in the story or of the story as a whole to find new understandings that you can share with your congregation.

For example, in the parable of the prodigal son, the younger son asks his father for an advance on his inheritance. This request was the equivalent of the son's telling his father that he wished he were dead. It showed the utmost disrespect. In the culture of that time, the father would have been justified in disowning or even killing his son for making such a request.

Later in the story, the father is said to have run to meet his returning son. This also is very unusual. In that culture, men of his social status never ran.

There are many books that shed light on Middle Eastern culture and customs. Some of my favorites were written by Kenneth E. Bailey.

Second, shed light on an obscure story. Some biblical passages are preached about time and time again; but there are others that are neglected. When was the last time you heard someone present Judah and Tamar's story (see Genesis 38)? How often is the book of Zephaniah the basis of a sermon? Recently, I preached on Shimei's cursing David (2 Samuel 16), bringing to light how David released resentment and offered forgiveness.

Remember, Paul advised a young preacher of his day that "all Scripture is God-breathed and is useful for teaching, rebuking, correcting and training in righteousness, so that the servant of God may be thoroughly equipped for every good work" (2 Timothy 3:16, 17).

Third, preach on an outstanding story that will stay in people's minds. Don't be afraid to use videos, dramatizations, or visual aids in your preaching as long as they support the sermon's message without overshadowing it.

6. Limit your preaching to about thirty minutes or less

Do you try to fit too much into the ideal time? Or do you say too little, using empty phrases and repetition to fill your thirty minutes? Are you serving empty calories or nutritious, satisfying food?

If you preach for more than thirty minutes, you're probably preaching too long. I don't know many people who say, "I wish he would preach a little longer." My wife always tells me when I preach to finish before the congregation wants me to finish. That's great advice.

5. Preach to two people

Preach to the person in your audience who's hearing for the first time what preaching is. This will make you seeker-friendly. It will help you view what you're saying from the point of view of the listeners who might not be familiar with our Christian jargon. There are many catchphrases that are like shortcuts to deep truths for those of us who have learned what they mean. What are shortcuts to us are dead-end roads to people who are hearing their first sermon. Think, for instance, of *fall on the Rock, the blood of the Lamb, justification, sanctification, glorification, I lift my Ebenezer,* and so on. And we Adventists have a lot of jargon unique to us, such as terms like "the Spirit of Prophecy," acronyms such as *NAD, SDA, GC,* and the list goes on.

Recently, I asked a seminary class of about thirty students if they knew the meaning of some of these phrases and acronyms. Most of these people had gone through the undergraduate courses required for their degrees and were now in graduate classes in that subject. Yet even they didn't know the full meaning of some of these phrases and acronyms, so it would be foolish to assume that every person in your congregation knows exactly what you are trying to convey when you use such terms. If people don't know the meaning of a word you're using, they're more likely to ignore what they're missing rather than to struggle to figure out what you're trying to say.

Be aware also that preparing a seeker-friendly sermon is more than just a matter of using the right vocabulary. It also means taking the time to make sure that your message is engaging and relevant to individuals of all walks of life. You should find ways to help the listeners understand in plain terms the hope of the gospel.

The other person to whom you need to preach to each Sabbath is the one who is hearing a sermon for the *last* time. Think through your sermon from the point of view of someone who's struggling with a boss who doesn't want to let that person have the Sabbath off. Think also of the possibility that a disease or accident may strike a member of your congregation. Don't run the risk of neglecting to give such persons the opportunity to renew their commitment to God. Keeping this person in mind will give urgency to what you say and to how you say it. It will drive you to make an appropriate appeal for acceptance of the Lord Jesus Christ and submission to Him.

4. Be honest and transparent

Show your integrity in all areas of your preaching. If you borrowed a joke or anecdote from the *Reader's Digest,* don't try to "personalize" it by pretending it happened to you or to someone you know. Comedians can get away with that, but ministers can't afford to lose their credibility.

People are most likely to think a preacher is credible when the sermon's truth has gripped the preacher. Listeners can tell when preachers don't believe their own sermons. So, preachers must not only know the subject but also believe it. When they do, their sermons will seep deep into their life and get ahold of them. This brings about conviction, repentance, and change.

It is healthy and helpful for the preacher to model this. However, preachers should avoid making the sermon hour into a show about their failings. If this happens, their confessions would become problematic distractions. Be gripped by the truth, and show how it grips you; but don't let all your sermons be confessions.

The most effective ministers are those whose relationship with God shows in all their life. They are gentle people who, however firmly they may speak, temper their words with kindness and love.

3. Give hope

It may be tempting to focus your sermons on guilt, shame, negativity, rebukes, manipulation, and the dark side of life and of current events. But to dwell on these trials and challenges is to ignore the hope we have in Jesus. Ellen White recounted her experience with a preacher who focused more on tribulation than on the love of God.

At Minneapolis we met a large delegation of ministers. I discerned at the very commencement of the meeting a spirit which burdened me. Discourses were preached that did not give the people the food which they so much needed. The dark and gloomy side of the picture was presented before them to hang in memory's hall. This would bring no light and spiritual freedom, but discouragement.

I felt deeply moved by the Spirit of the Lord Sabbath afternoon [Oct. 13, 1888] to call the minds of those present to the love God manifests to His people. The mind must not be permitted to dwell on the most objectionable features of our faith. In God's Word, which may be represented as a garden filled with roses and lilies and pinks, we may pluck by faith the precious promises of God, appropriate them to our own hearts, and be of good courage—yes, joyful in God—or we may keep our attention fastened on the briars and thistles and wound ourselves severely and bemoan our hard lot.

God is not pleased to have His people hanging dark and painful pictures in memory's hall. He would have every soul plucking the roses and the lilies and the pinks, hanging memory's hall with the precious promises of God blooming all over the garden of God. He would have us dwelling upon them, our senses sharp and clear, taking them in in their full richness, talking of the joy that is set before us. He would have us living in the world yet not of it, our affections taking hold of eternal things. He would have us talking of the things which He has prepared for those that love Him. This will attract our minds, awaken our hopes and expectations, and strengthen our souls to endure the conflicts and trials of this life. As we dwell on these scenes the Lord will encourage our faith and confidence. He will draw aside the veil and give us glimpses of the saints' inheritance.[2]

Jesus, through His ministry of healing and teaching, made it a point to share the hope and grace of His Father everywhere He went. We would be wise to do the same. "Hope does not put us to shame, because God's love has been poured out into our hearts through the Holy Spirit, who has been given to us" (Romans 5:5).

2. Preach in the power of the Holy Spirit

We have no right to preach the Word of God until we have first been anointed by the Spirit of God (see Acts 1:4, 5, 8). After heaven's anointing at Pentecost, the followers of Jesus went out to preach in the power of the Holy Spirit. When Stephen—who was "full of faith and the Holy Spirit"—preached, his hearers "were not able to resist the wisdom and the Spirit by which he spoke." Even Stephen's nonverbal communication was an irrefutable witness: "All who sat in the council, looking steadfastly at him, saw his face as the face of an angel" (Acts 6:5, 10, 15). Stephen's life demonstrated that when preachers are filled with the Holy Spirit, they are full of power.

We can ask for the indwelling of the Holy Spirit with confidence because Jesus said, "If you then, though you are evil, know how to give good gifts to your children, how much more will your Father in heaven give the Holy Spirit to those who ask him!" (Luke 11:13). We too can declare with boldness that "the Spirit of the Lord is upon me because He has anointed me to preach" (Luke 4:18, NKJV).

1. Bathe your sermon preparation and delivery in prayer

Jesus, the Master Preacher, devoted large amounts of time to prayer. As He prepared to preach in the synagogues throughout Galilee, He rose early in the morning, went to a solitary place, and prayed (Mark 1:35–39). And before Jesus preached His sermon on the bread of life, He spent hours in prayer (Matthew 14:23–25). Jesus believed that preaching and prayer were intricately connected.

The disciples of Jesus realized that those who minister the Word must also devote themselves to prayer (see Acts 6:4). The many days that the followers of Jesus spent in intense seasons of prayer prior to Pentecost were not only an essential preparation for the Spirit's anointing but were also an essential preparation for powerful preaching. The apostle Paul affirmed the importance of prayer in sermon preparation and delivery when he made the special request for intercessory prayer "that utterance may be given to me, that I may open my mouth boldly to make known the mystery of the gospel" (Ephesians 6:19, NKJV). He understood that without prayer he could not "speak boldly, as I ought to speak" (verse 20, NKJV).

The dearth of powerful biblical preaching that we sometimes experience can be rectified by powerful praying. Peter's denial of Jesus illustrates the troubling truth that we will have no powerful testimony about Jesus to share with others if we have been sleeping when we should have been praying. The lesson is clear. Pray for God's guidance before you begin to prepare your sermon. Pray for it while you prepare it. And pray for it while you preach it. Learn from the example of Jesus that there is power in our preaching when we pray. Bathe your sermon preparation and delivery in prayer.

The suggestions I've given in these two chapters are things you can do right away to strengthen your preaching immediately. As I look back on the sermons I have preached that have seemed to have the most traction, I see that the majority of them are sermons in which I faithfully unfolded the passage and then have gotten out of the way and let Jesus shine.

Here's a recent example of how this has worked for me. I was to be a guest speaker for a vespers service at Andrews University. I prayed for several weeks that God would help me in my preparation and study, giving me an inspiring message that would open the heart of someone listening and encourage them to ask me for Bible studies. My sermon was focused on the fact that we can forgive others through the power of God, who has forgiven us.

After the service, a young woman and her parents approached me. They had been touched by my words, and over the next half hour they shared their story. They were visiting their daughter and had come to the vespers service only at her insistence. They had stopped going to church because of a conflict with other members of the congregation, but that night their hearts had been softened as they were reminded of the forgiveness that God gives us, and they determined to forgive those who had offended them and return to church. I thanked God for allowing me to see how His message was touching lives. I saw this as an answer to my prayer.

However, as I was heading to my car, another young woman called to me, saying she had been waiting for me to come out of the church and wanted to talk with me. She was a new student at Andrews, but she was attending there only because there'd been issues with the university that was her first choice.

This young woman told me she didn't know anything about God, Christianity, or the Bible. She said she was so touched by the message I gave that she wanted to learn more—she wanted to have Bible studies. Those studies led to her baptism and acceptance of Christ. I thank the Lord that He answered my prayer so specifically and gave me the words to say that would show Jesus to someone in need.

Experiences such as this encourage me to continue spending time in preparation and prayer and in increasing my skill as a preacher. They also show me the power with which the Word of God convicts hearts. "The word of God is alive and active. Sharper than any double-edged sword, it penetrates even to dividing soul and spirit" (Hebrews 4:12). "Faith comes from hearing the message, and the message is heard through the word about Christ" (Romans 10:17).

---

1. White, *Gospel Workers,* 158, 159.

2. Ellen G. White, *Selected Messages,* book 3 (Washington, D.C.: Review and Herald®, 1958, 1980), 163, 164.

Chapter 12
Planning a Sermonic Year

"Everything should be done in a fitting and orderly way."—*1 Corinthians 14:40*

Even though developing a sermonic year is a long process, it is essential to achieving the mission of the church. It is the result of the collective philosophy, mission, and vision of the church. It gives direction and inspiration to the members and focus to the pastor and lay leaders.[1]

When I was pastoring, I would plan a sermonic calendar year that ran from January to December. Before I could begin planning it, however, I had to spend three to five hours each week from August to October preparing for the planning stage. Much of that time I was praying for wisdom and the leading of the Holy Spirit. I needed to hear from God where He wanted me to lead my church in the upcoming year.

How to create a sermonic-year master calendar

A sermonic-year master calendar is a tool that enables both the pastor and the church's ministry teams to stay organized. It also helps the pastor and the lay leadership of the church to determine whether the spiritual diet they've prepared to nourish the congregation during the approaching year is balanced in presenting various themes. This enables them to make sure that the programs they're planning for the new year are in line with the mission God has for the church. Here are some steps to take to develop a sermonic-year calendar:

1. Survey the community and the congregation. The first step is to survey the community to discover what topics interest the unchurched. Be sure to involve your leadership team and the lay members of the church in this process. One way to do this is to go to a few neighborhood shops and ask patrons what topics they would like to hear if they were to come to church. Another way is to have your members reach out to family and friends to find out what they would like to hear from a church.

I always made sure that I had a series of sermons that were suggested by nonmembers, and I'd send flyers advertising them. I noted that the members of the community requested the subject I was advertising. This created credibility and brought some new people to the church. Among the subjects they suggested were how to raise kids, how to have a better marriage, what the New Age is, and why there are so many religions. Getting feedback from seekers helps you to focus on the needs of the unchurched and to be intentional about reaching them.

But don't ignore the members of your congregation. Find out what they would like you to address, and allow them to suggest topics of interest.

2. Hold a leadership retreat. Every August I held a spiritual/planning weekend retreat for the church's leadership team. We spent Friday night and most of Sabbath praying, worshiping, reading the Bible, and reflecting. Then we spent Saturday night and Sunday morning visioning the future. During that time I learned much from the leadership team about the needs of the congregation and the community and the direction my programming and my sermonic year should take. We also used this time to hammer out dates for special events, such as VBS, and to see whether there were programs we'd had during the previous year that were no longer effective and shouldn't be put on the calendar.

During that weekend I received valuable feedback from the team on what they felt the church needed. There were issues and challenges in the congregation and community that they made me aware of that hadn't been brought up in the surveys. The leaders shared their perspectives of the church as a whole as well as their individual concerns. Much of what they said gave me insights into the spiritual pulse of the leaders and the church, and that told me a lot about the strengths and weaknesses of the church, determining the content of the sermonic year.

3. Pray, study, and reflect. When we returned from the retreat, I spent considerable time in prayer, Bible study, and reflection contemplating the needs of the church and where I felt God was leading us. Sometimes I felt He was calling us to a greater focus on mission. Other times it seemed He wanted us to build community and to deal with various topics such as personal sanctification and spiritual growth. I took all of these ideas and placed them on a spreadsheet so I could see the connections between them and make a logical sequence from them.

4. Put together a first draft. By October, I had finished working on a first draft of the master calendar and the upcoming sermonic year. At this point, I placed everything that I was planning on a one-page calendar so I could see the whole year at a glance. Here are some things I've found should be included:

- All the major events of the year, paying close attention to the seasonal events: New Year's Day, Valentine's Day, Easter, Mother's Day, Father's

Day, Thanksgiving Day, and Christmas. People are more inclined to go to church on these special days than just about any other time. So it's wise to use the opportunities provided by these days to invite them to worship with you again.

- Other days that were special to my church, such as its anniversary (to emphasize how God led in the past and His vision for the future), vacation times, school breaks, VBS, and two short evangelistic meetings—one to be conducted in February, and one in September. Each of these evangelistic series spanned a week and two weekends.[2] The special Sabbaths in this item plus those in the preceding one occupy fourteen to eighteen weeks of the year.
- The overall rhythm of the church.

5. Schedule Communion services. I put Communion and footwashing on the calendar four times a year. I tried to make sure we conducted one (or more) of them on a Friday night or Saturday night so we could have an agape feast to give variety to our celebration of the ordinances.

6. Work in acts of kindness. In conjunction with a sermon series on action, I always planned four Sabbath afternoons of service to the community. During these Sabbaths people could engage in any form of community service that appealed to them, whether individually or with other people.

7. Schedule Rewind Sabbaths. We also had two "Rewind" Sabbaths a year around the beginning of December. On those days we thank the Lord for how He has led us. During that time:

- We have all the people who were baptized in the past year and all those who were instrumental in their conversion give their testimonies.
- Through testimonies and videos, we highlight all of the ministries God empowered the church to carry out during the past year.
- I give summaries of all the series I've preached during the year and emphasize their relevancy and application.

8. Schedule the sermon series you'll have during the next year. Look for blocks of Sabbaths on your calendar that will accommodate sermon series that are four to eight weeks long. Series that are shorter won't have the optimum impact, and series that are longer bore people.

Leave one to three weeks open between each series. That way the pastoral staff can address current events and issues, bring in a guest speaker,[3] or make the series a bit longer if the Spirit so moves. Be sure to take into consideration the series length necessitated by the theme you are planning to present. And be prepared to interrupt the series for a week if circumstances make that necessary.

9. Get feedback and then make your final draft. At this point, I give the nearly finished calendar to the board members, church secretary, musicians, graphic designer, outreach coordinator, and anyone else who needs to know our plans for the year ahead. I do this to get feedback from the leadership team, but passing it out at this stage is also a matter of publicity. Everyone knows what the church will be doing in the coming year and can participate.

When I have incorporated the feedback from the leadership team and have made sure that they are comfortable with the schedule, I give the final version of the calendar to all the church members. I do this by November so the members can make their plans and invite friends and family to the series that will be of interest to them.

How to plan a sermon series

A sermon series consists of two or more sermons that develop a single theme or cover a single subject. Preachers may choose to use sermon series for several reasons, among them to provide the time to cover a complex subject adequately or to undercut prejudice by exposure. Generally, the sermons that comprise the series are presented consecutively, though sometimes the preacher may interrupt it for a week or two. To develop a sermon series that accomplishes what you intend it to, you must first prayerfully choose major themes to address. Every topic on which you preach falls into one of the following categories:

- Felt needs, which covers all of the "how-tos," such as raising kids God's way, overcoming depression, handling anger, or breaking bad habits.
- Spiritual growth, which includes topics such as prayer, Bible study, worship, sanctification, and justification.
- Doctrines, which are covered during evangelistic meetings.
- Stewardship, which includes the four "T"s: tithe (and offering), temple (your body), talents, and time.
- Vision casting, which includes the journey the church is going on, both spiritually and relationally, toward embodying the character of the first-century church of Acts 2.
- Seasonal.

Don't limit yourself to just one or two of these themes. Try to find room in your calendar to touch on all of the above categories. Because it usually takes four to eight weeks to cover each of these, you'll need about two years to cover all of them.

For example, I dealt with my vision, values, and mission for the church in January of every year. I addressed stewardship in April and "seasonally" throughout the year as the seasons came and went. For instance, I would deal with the life and teachings of Jesus around Easter and marriage and parenting around Mother's Day.

Second, be sure to balance your sermons so you have a good mix. Base some on the Old Testament, some on the New, with some being topical or thematic sermons. Some of the books of the Bible, such as Genesis and John, provide "inroads" to so many topics that they can be used to lead into almost every category listed above. Help your people get deeper into the Word. Regardless of the theme you are sharing, every sermon should also reflect the gospel message.

Sometimes we gave the whole year a theme, such as "The Year of Mission." In that case, I tied every sermon series to what it means to be missional. Many of the series were overtly about mission, such as "The Most Effective Evangelist in the World" and the Holy Spirit's role in mission. There was also a series on James with the central theme "If we're going to be a church on a mission, then our best missional testimony is how we live."

Other times, we decided that each month or sermon series needed its own theme. For example, the whole month of November could deal with thankfulness, or we could use Mother's Day to speak to the parental characteristics of God.

Some themes[4] to consider are the character of God, spiritual disciplines, denominational distinctiveness, Christian basics, Bible characters, and the Ten Commandments.

How to craft a sermon series

Preaching a series of sermons on a topic or on a passage of Scripture allows you to develop a theme more thoroughly than is possible in a single sermon. That means you can also give it more impact. But a sermon series demands more from the preacher in the way of "packaging" than a stand-alone sermon does. You must divide the topic or passage into pieces you can cover each week. Keep your sermons simple enough for seekers to understand without diluting your message. Avoid jargon, and explain the theological terms you use. Choose a title, subtitle, and text for the entire series, with titles for the individual sermons—perhaps finding a metaphor with which you can tie the sermons together.

Once you know the blocks of time you can use, schedule each sermon series on your calendar and then begin to plan the order of the individual sermons. Try building a progression in which your sermons move from the theological to the practical—in other words, from the *why* to the *what*. This way you are leading people toward personal and corporate application of the spiritual truths they have learned.

Before you preach any of the sermons in your series, develop a creative team that includes worship leaders, media directors, elders, and a couple of other creative people. Take a day or a few evenings and work on the series in broad brush strokes, talking about the overarching metaphors and ideas you want to communicate.

The role of the team is to help flesh out the ideas. They need to be honest enough to say things like, "I think if you preach it that way, you will deliver the theological goods, but I don't think that will change anybody's heart." If some of your team says something like that, take their comments seriously, go back to the drawing board, and do some more work. Always ask, "How is this truly going to change lives?"

Creative teams are beneficial not only because they give honest feedback but also because they keep you working ahead. When you work ahead, you become more creative, and good ideas eventually become great ones. And team members can help with illustrations, PowerPoint slides, videos, titles, etc.

Once you've established the flow of the sermon series, you should begin work on branding. That means you must determine the vocabulary and the images that you will use to communicate the message of the series. For example, we titled a series on the Holy Spirit "3rd Person" and chose titles and graphics that reflect the mystery of the Spirit. We also branded a series on the Bible by giving it the title "TXT MSG."

Planning your sermonic year with intentionality means you can avoid the panic that comes from not knowing what you will be preaching about next week. It means you'll have time for the worship and communication coordinators to plan services and branding that will contribute to the theme and allows for a balance in the topics and spiritual lessons presented.[5] It also inspires people to see whether there's a way they can begin to incorporate ministry initiatives into the way they live.

Remember, you aren't trying to produce creative branding in order to make people think you're clever. You are working to show that the Bible is relevant. If we aren't handling the Word of God with integrity and showing people how truth will make a difference in their lives, all our creativity is nothing more than smoke and mirrors. In the end, we hit the mark when we preach God's Word in a way that opens our hearers to genuine transformation.

Use the sermonic year as a tool to bring edification to the members of your church and to further God's mission.

---

1. A sermonic-year calendar can be effective for those who pastor in multichurch districts too, but making one work may require your elders and guest preachers to preach to themes you give them rather than picking their own topics. For more information about planning with church districts in mind, see Rodlie Ortiz, "Planning a Preaching Calendar for a Multichurch District," *Ministry* 83, no. 8 (August 2011): 13, 14, https://www.ministrymagazine.org/archive/2011/08 /planning-a-preaching-calendar-for-a-multichurch-district.

2. One of these could be extended to a full evangelistic series spanning three or four weeks.

3. I don't invite guest speakers in order to fill time at the eleven o'clock hour on Sabbath mornings. I invite them to help me fulfill my vision and mission for the church. I might invite some guest speakers for training purposes, others for evangelistic purposes, and yet others because they have a big name and will draw a crowd.

4. For more theme ideas, see J. Reynolds Hoffman, "Planning a Sermonic Year," *Ministry* 51, no. 12 (December 1978): 8, 9, https://www.ministrymagazine.org/archive/1978/12/planning-a-sermonic-year.

5. For further insights see Derek Morris, "From Panic to Purpose: The Process and Benefits of Planning a Preaching Calendar," *Ministry* 76, no. 9 (September 2004): 30, 31, https://www.ministrymagazine.org/archive/2004/09/from-panic-to-purpose.html.

Section Five
Church Planting

Church planting is an effective evangelistic tool that, unfortunately, too many people overlook. The research I did for the first chapter in this section, "Insights Gained From Planting Churches," indicates that here in North America we are not planting as many churches as we should be—and consequently, we are failing to grow as rapidly as earth's population is. Ellen White challenges us: "The people who bear [God's] sign are to establish churches and institutions as memorials to Him."*

In part, we aren't doing enough church planting because of the many myths we've heard about the challenges that befall those who use this approach. In the second chapter of this section, I raise three of the myths about this evangelistic method, and I cut away the misperceptions and reveal the truth. In this chapter, I also present some simple things you can do to get your church started planting churches. Even though the research conducted for this section was done in North America, the implications are universal.

---

* White, *Testimonies for the Church,* 7:105.

Chapter 13
Lessons Learned From Planting Churches[1]

"This gospel of the kingdom will be preached in the whole world as a testimony to all nations, and then the end will come."—Matthew 24:14

"Upon all who believe, God has placed the burden of raising up churches." —Ellen G. White[2]

At the inception of the Advent movement, clusters of Adventists united to advance the cause of the gospel by moving to places where there were no Adventists and raising up congregations. This approach produced explosive growth that eventually enabled the church to spread around the world. Now it is time to ask whether we are establishing enough new congregations to give us the assurance that we will complete the harvest in North America. To answer this question, we decided to review statistics that picture the progress of Seventh-day Adventist church planting. We hope that the findings from this study will benefit our church not only in North America but also around the world, where in some areas, it is growing rapidly and in others it is struggling.[3]

The North American Division (NAD) comprises the members of the Seventh-day Adventist Church in Bermuda, Canada, and the United States. The following graph compares the growth in the number of Adventist churches in these three countries over the past one hundred years with the growth of those countries' population during that time span.[4]

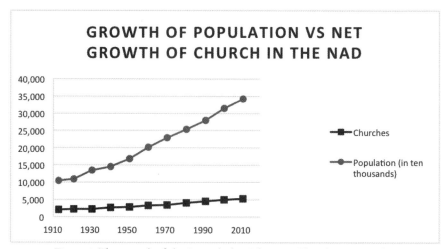

Figure 1. The growth of the Seventh-day Adventist Church in Bermuda, Canada, and the United States as compared to the growth of the population of these countries.

In 1913, there were 2,006 Adventist churches in the NAD to fulfill Jesus' commission of carrying the Adventist message to the 105 million people that comprised the population of these three countries. By 2011, these numbers had changed. By that time there were 5,332 churches carrying the message to the 342 million people in the NAD. In other words, in 1913, the ratio of Adventist churches to total population was one church for every 52,000 people. By 2011, the ratio had increased to one church for every 64,000 people.

This data confronts the Seventh-day Adventist Church in North America with a staggering reality: *we are not planting churches rapidly enough to keep up with population growth.* The existing Adventist churches alone will never be able to keep up with the fast-growing population, especially in areas with no current Adventist presence. In other words, over the past century the challenge of evangelizing the territory of the NAD has grown rather than decreased.

However, reaching this burgeoning population is not impossible. In the past century, the number of Adventist churches in North America has grown by 1.03 percent per year. This number fits church growth expert Lyle Schaller's 1 Percent Rule. He says that denominations cannot avoid declining by maintaining the number of churches they currently have. Because of the growth of the population—just to maintain the current ratio of their churches per the population of their territory, they must add 1 percent more each year. To grow faster than the general population, they must, every year, plant 2 to 3 percent *more* churches than currently exist.[5]

Figure 2 portrays what would happen if one of every four churches planted a daughter church each decade. To illustrate this in the Adventist context over the past century, we projected a 2.5 percent growth rate in the number of churches per year (25 percent per decade).[6]

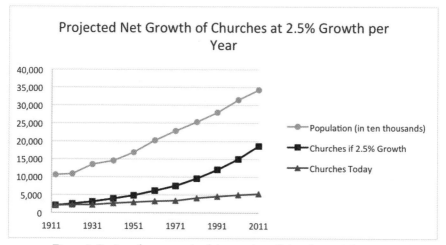

Figure 2. Projected net growth of the number of churches at 2.5 percent growth per year.

Figure 2 shows that if we had adopted the 2.5 percent rule, by 2011 we would have had more than three times as many churches—18,682—as we actually had, and the ratio of Adventist churches to population would have increased to one per 18,000. In other words, through planting more churches, Seventh-day Adventists can improve the ratio of churches to population. Ratios are important because they reveal the number of people a church needs to influence to have a role in fulfilling the Great Commission. In other words, ratios identify the size of the mission field of each church.

Dan Serns, who has planted at least one church in every district he has pastored in Texas, Kansas, and Washington and who now pastors the Richardson Seventh-day Adventist Church in Texas, says new congregations are essential to expanding the influence of the church for the kingdom of God. His vision is a vibrant Seventh-day Adventist congregation for every ten thousand people.[7] This is in harmony with what Kevin Ezell discovered in his study of the Southern Baptist denomination. The church thrives when the ratio of churches to population climbs to or exceeds one per ten thousand.[8]

Research regarding the ratios of Adventist churches per population for each decade that our study covered revealed that while there were some decades in which the church succeeded in lowering the ratio, its general trend has been to fall behind. (See figure 3.)

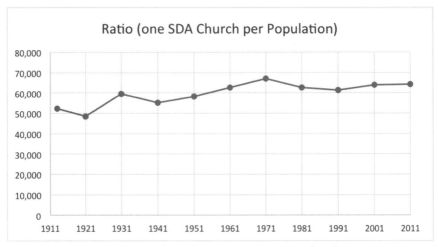

**Figure 3. The ratio of Seventh-day Adventist churches
per population size through a century.**

Examination of the above data reveals the following:

- The best ratio was reached in 1921: one church per 48,500 people.
- The worst ratio the church experienced was in 1971: one church per 67,000 people.
- The ratio improved during four decades: 1913–1921, 1931–1941, 1971–1981, and 1981–1991.
- The worst ratio in history (1971) was counteracted by a massive church-planting movement that began in the 1970s and continued into the 1980s.
- The ratio in 2011 (the last year of our study)[9] was one church per 64,000 people.
- The 2011 ratio is much closer to the worst it's ever been than to the best.

In the 1970s,[10] the Adventist Church made great strides in church planting, which resulted in its recovery from the low point it reached in 1971. We need another massive church-planting movement today. Established churches must be moved to plant churches that will, in turn, also plant new churches. Ellen White counseled, "As churches are established, it should be set before them that it is even from among them that men must be taken to carry the truth to others and raise new churches."[11] This paradigm shift must happen on all levels of the church. We believe that every pastor, administrator, member, conference, and church can be part of the solution.

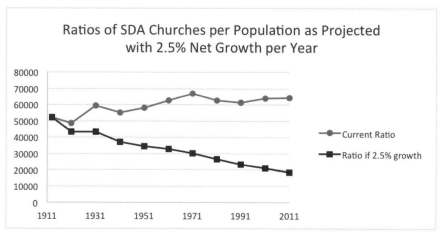

Figure 4. Ratios of Seventh-day Adventist churches per population as projected with 2.5 percent net growth per year.

Figure 4 shows that if the Seventh-day Adventist Church had planted churches at the rate of 2.5 percent per year, the number of people that each congregation would need to influence would be about 18,000. This is a more manageable goal for a congregation to reach, which means they can play a significant role in fulfilling the Great Commission in North America. But because we haven't planted churches at the appropriate rate, each congregation now is responsible for reaching 64,000 people.

Interpreting the data

For the past century, the North American Division has grown by an average of thirty-five churches per year. That is an average of about six churches per decade per conference. That means each conference has grown by about half (0.6) a church per year.

The data reveals that Seventh-day Adventist church planting in North America is an exception rather than an expectation. In the past decade, there was a net increase of 399 churches. If we assumed that each additional church came from a distinct mother church, that would suggest that only 8 percent of the churches in the NAD planted a church. That means 92 percent of churches in the NAD have not planted a church within the past ten years. So, the potential for growth is almost unlimited! If even an additional 8 percent planted churches this decade, the year 2021 would see nearly eight hundred new Adventist congregations faithfully sharing Jesus with thousands who desperately need Him. The harvest in North America desperately calls for every Adventist to be involved in a massive church-planting movement.

In order to reach Schaller's 2.5 percent growth-rate formula during the next decade in North America, we need to experience a net growth of 1,333 churches. That is an average of 133.3 churches per year. That is an average of 2.25 churches per conference per year. Moving from 0.60 to 2.25 churches per conference per year will require significant effort. However, this goal is very achievable considering that during the past decade, the top four conferences in church planting averaged 5.15 churches and companies per year (see the chart below). A massive church-planting movement in North America is definitely achievable.

Imagine a massive church-planting movement

In order to have a realistic picture of what a massive Adventist church-planting movement might look like, we first looked at a place where successful church planting was taking place in North America. Then, to keep our study to a manageable size, we identified the conferences doing the most and the best church planting in the past ten years.[12] Only four of the fifty-nine conferences showed a net increase of at least forty-five churches and companies during the time our study covered—an average of 4.5 or more per year. (See following table.)[13]

Table 1. The top four conferences in the NAD in church planting in the past decade and the number of churches and companies they planted.

Conference	Churches	Companies	Total
Texas	31	26	57
Georgia-Cumberland	22	31	53
Greater New York	40	8	48
Florida	13	35	48

For our study of the top four conferences, we drew from the General Conference archives and statistics, conference and church archives, and interviews conducted with conference officials, pastors, and lay leaders.

Renew or plant?

While doing our research, we discovered that one of the biggest roadblocks to increasing church planting is the many plateauing and declining Adventist churches in North America. Church-growth experts make the case that a lack of church planting is one of the major causes of decline.[14]

Ellen White has said that churches and members who are dying spiritually can experience renewal by bringing the Advent message to areas where there are no Adventists.[15] Renewal comes as church members focus on carrying out their mission, developing disciples, and taking great steps in faith. As the spirituality of the church members increases, they become more aware of the ripe fields around them and seek training (discipleship) and structure (ministry and churches planted) so they can harvest the ripe grain.[16]

Our study revealed that one of the best ways to bring about church renewal is through planting another church. We believe that with the power supplied by the Holy Spirit, any Adventist church—even one that was planted within the past ten years—can plant another church.

We didn't find any mother church that suffered because of planting a church. In fact, many examples showed that planting daughter churches renewed the mother churches and actually brought them more people and resources than they had before they planted a church.

For instance, the Hollywood (Florida) Spanish Seventh-day Adventist Church[17] was experiencing decline. The building in which they were meeting was a small, rented facility, and the congregation felt that they were stuck there for the future. Then they awoke to the needs around them. The leadership of the church began to emphasize mission and discipleship through preaching, education, and frequent reminders of the importance of reaching the community around them. The church members shifted their focus from the inward to the outward, and they decided that they were going to plant new congregations.

Allan Machado, Hispanic coordinator for the Florida Conference, told us that "as soon as they put their heart into mission, they started to grow and multiply."[18] An Adventist businessman saw God at work and bought the church a new five-million-dollar church building. But when they moved into the building, maintaining it just about bankrupted them. They decided to trust God and continue planting new churches anyway. During the next five years, they planted four churches and became a two-language (Spanish and English) church. As I write this, their membership is close to three hundred, and the combined membership of all five churches is about a thousand. Hollywood Spanish Seventh-day Adventist Church is one of many churches we studied that experienced renewal as the members stepped out in faith to plant a church.

The new movement
Beginning an Adventist church-planting movement in North America will require the participation of people on all levels of the church.

> There is a work for every mind and for every hand. There is a variety of work, adapted to different minds and varied capabilities. Everyone who is connected with God will impart light to others. . . .
> . . . If they will become co-laborers with Jesus, we shall see the light in our churches steadily burning brighter and brighter, sending forth its rays to penetrate the darkness beyond their own borders.[19]

Our study of the top four conferences in church planting revealed that there are a variety of models that work. Dr. Gerson Santos, vice president of the Greater New York Conference, noted, "The city is so diverse, that I don't think we can have just one model." The following models were used by the top four conferences of the past decade. They illustrate that people at every level of the church can play a role in a massive church-planting movement.

1. Member initiated. Church members start small groups in their homes. They meet during the week and witness in their community. As the groups grow and multiply, anywhere from one to four of the groups combine and begin meeting together on Sabbath mornings for worship.

Though this church plant starts as a Seventh-day Adventist group, it may not be directly connected to any particular Adventist church at first. But eventually it works with a "foster" mother church or directly with the conference as it organizes as a church.

2. Mother-church initiated. The mother-church-initiated church plant may take one or more of many forms.

- A mother church chooses a leader and a core group from within their congregation to plant a daughter church.
- Two or more churches work together to plant a daughter church.
- A mother church plants a church by starting a new worship service either at the same facility or at some other location with the goal of reaching people with a different demographic than most of members of the mother church.
- A well-endowed Sabbath School class may grow into becoming a church plant.
- Members of a church that speak one language plant a church for people who speak another language (e.g., a Spanish-speaking church plants a church for people who speak English).
- A church with a mostly elderly membership hosts or plants a youth or children's church.

3. Conference initiated.

- The conference focuses on an area where there is little or no Adventist presence and sponsors a church planter to begin working there.
- A conference works with a lay pastor to establish a new church.
- A conference or group of conferences creates a center of influence from which to reach a city. For example, the Greater New York Conference converted an Adventist Book Center downtown into a juice bar café

where people meet to have a Bible study and fellowship at lunchtime on weekdays and worship services on Sabbath.

These are a few of many examples of ways that every level of the church can get involved in a church-planting movement. A thread of commonality ran through the four conferences and the churches we studied—they were raised up so they could carry out the mission God has given to us. Successful church plants come out of a mission-driven consciousness, not out of conflict or dissension. All four conferences were very intentional, having allocated conference personnel and resources to the project and having developed strategic plans for doing it.

In our study, we discovered a correlation between church planting and membership growth. The top four conferences in church planting from 2001 to 2011 were above the NAD average in membership growth (NAD: 1.8 percent per year, compared to Texas, with 4.2 percent; Georgia-Cumberland, 2.8 percent; Greater New York, 2.4 percent; and Florida, 2 percent). The numbers per year of baptisms and professions of faith that the top four conferences attained are evidence of the connection between church planting and evangelism (Texas: 2,279; Georgia-Cumberland: 1,130; Greater New York: 1,369, and Florida: 2,365). All four conferences saw church planting as an invaluable key for reaching the harvest. (See table 2.)

Table 2. The percentage of growth and the number of baptisms of the top four conferences in the NAD for church planting in the past decade.

Conference	Growth	Baptisms
Texas	4.2%	2,279
Georgia Cumberland	2.8%	1,130
Greater New York	2.4%	1,369
Florida	2.0%	2,365

Recurring themes and some lessons we learned

Our interviews and research uncovered some major recurring themes. Here are some of the lessons we learned about church planting:

First, *doing* something *is better than doing nothing*. Merely starting a new small group or even just talking about planting a church is a step forward. Once the concept has gained some momentum, you can work to identify and mentor potential leaders.

Second, *church planting is a result of making disciples*. As people grow in their passion for God, they need new opportunities to use their energy and abilities in witness and service. A church plant provides abundant opportunities for involvement in ministry.

Third, *lay-led planting is more common, more effective, and more affordable.* The greatest investment you can make toward increasing church planting is in the development of the spirituality and leadership abilities of a few key people.

Fourth, *church planting creates synergy for both mother and daughter churches.* Focusing on the mission and building new leaders brings renewal to the mother church and equips the daughter church. Churches that plant other churches receive rich blessings and grow in numbers, health, and finances.

Fifth, *conferences that implement an intentional church-planting strategy experience significant growth.* Effective strategies include appointing a church-planting coordinator for the conference, recruiting and training lay leaders, coaching church planters, utilizing demographics studies, and allocating funds for special church-planting projects.

The Seventh-day Adventist Church sprang up as a movement that had the goal of fulfilling the Great Commission by entering new territory and raising up new congregations. However, in North America the church-planting movement has been largely forgotten. The challenge of reaching the rapidly growing population in North America is great, but through the power of the Holy Spirit and intentionality on all levels of the church, we can reach these people.

Planting new churches is essential for the growth and vitality of the Adventist Church in all parts of the world. Every new church is a visible monument to God's love for humanity and is able to reach distinct people groups and communities with the everlasting gospel. Developing a massive church-planting movement is daunting, but even a small step in that direction can be effective when multiplied by the power of the Holy Spirit.[20]

---

1. Dustin Serns, Master of Divinity graduate from the Seventh-day Adventist Theological Seminary at Andrews University, aided in the writing of this chapter.

2. Ellen G. White, *Medical Ministry* (Mountain View, Calif.: Pacific Press®, 1932), 315.

3. For example, from 2001 to 2011, the Southern Asia Division grew by 8.1 percent in churches and companies per year, and the South American Division grew by 4.9 percent per year. During that period, the General Conference as a whole grew by 3 percent in churches and companies per year. Information accessed January 20, 2014, from the Seventh-day Adventist Church Office of Archives, Statistics, and Research Web site at http://www.adventiststatistics.org.

4. Population estimates taken from "Population Estimates," United States Census Bureau, accessed September 20, 2013, http://www.census.gov/popest/data/index.html; "Overpopulation in Your State," Negative Population Growth, accessed September 20, 2013, http://www.npg.org /facts/us_historical_pops.htm; Statistics Canada, accessed September 20, 2013, http://www .statcan.gc.ca/start-debut-eng.html; "Population of Canada," *Wikipedia,* accessed October 10, 2013, http://en.wikipedia.org/wiki/Population_of_Canada_by_year; and "Burmuda Demographics Profile 2014," index mundi, accessed October 10, 2013, http://www.indexmundi.com /bermuda/demographics_profile.html.

All church statistics come from the Seventh-day Adventist Church Office of Archives, Statistics, and Research at http://www.adventiststatistics.org. We arrived at the net growth of churches by subtracting the churches that close or merge from the total church plants.

We did not include Seventh-day Adventist companies in order to remain consistent because of insufficient data. In 1913, the denomination reported the number of churches and companies, but from 1914 to 1996 the numbers of companies were not recorded in the official archives. Although a few individuals point out that there are some companies of considerable size in the NAD, we see this fact offset by the significant number of very small churches.

5. Lyle E. Schaller, *44 Questions for Church Planters* (Nashville, Tenn.: Abingdon, 1991), 12.

6. A contemporary example of this growth rate from the world church in the last decade of our study (2001–2011) is that of the Inter-American Division, which experienced a 2.4 percent increase in churches and companies per year. During that period the membership grew from 2,078,226 to 3,403,718, or 6.4 percent per year. This illustrates the correlation between church planting and membership growth.

7. Dan Serns, telephone interview, November 15, 2013.

8. North American Mission Board, "Why We Need More Churches," Whatever It Takes, accessed November 25, 2013, http://www.namb.net/Population__Church_Ratios/.

9. The most recent year available with full church statistics at the time of this research was 2011.

10. For extensive church-planting research conducted through the 1970s and 1980s, see Roger Dudley and Clarence Gruesbeck, *Plant a Church, Reap a Harvest* (Boise, Idaho: Pacific Press®, 1989). Monte Sahlin also adds that one of the significant reasons for growth in church planting during that time was the church's response to the rise of immigrant groups in North America and the importance of addressing their needs (telephone interview, October 10, 2013). This is an illustration of an intentional church-planting movement that aims to reach the ever-growing population.

11. White, *Testimonies for the Church*, 3:205. Ed Stetzer affirms this principle, calling for churches not only to plant daughter churches but to aim to become "grandparent churches." *Viral Churches: Helping Church Planters Become Movement Makers* (San Francisco: Jossey-Bass, 2010), 31–47.

12. Research drawn from the Seventh-day Adventist Church Office of Archives, Statistics, and Research Web site at http://www.adventiststatistics.org. The most current results available measured from 2001 to 2011.

13. Statistics taken October 10, 2013, from the Seventh-day Adventist Church Office of Archives, Statistics, and Research at http://www.adventiststatistics.org.

14. Aubrey Malphurs argues that church planting is the key to survival as a denomination in *Planting Growing Churches for the 21st Century* (Grand Rapids, Mich.: Baker, 2004), 32–38. Lyle Schaller makes the case that the lack of church planting is one major cause of the decline of mainline Protestantism in *44 Questions for Church Planters,* 24–26. The same scenario is true for Adventism.

15. White, *Testimonies for the Church*, 8:244.

16. For more details on simple strategic steps to take toward church planting, see chapter 14, "From Obstacles to Opportunities."

17. For examples of this principle from other ethnic demographics, see chapter 14, "From Obstacles to Opportunities."

18. Allan Machado, telephone interview, October 22, 2013.

19. Ellen G. White, *Notebook Leaflets From the Elmshaven Library* (Washington, D.C.: Review and Herald®, 1945), 1:27.

20. Church planting is a difficult endeavor. Claiming territory for Jesus most certainly solicits opposition from many sides. Those who commit to church planting encounter significant obsta-

cles, but as they depend on God, He answers with incredible blessings and rewards. The following chapter will address three major obstacles to church planting based on data and interviews from the top four conferences in church planting.

Inspired Insights on Church Planting
From Ellen G. White

"Upon all who believe, God has placed the burden of raising up churches." —*Medical Ministry*, 315.

"New churches must be established, new congregations organized. At this time there should be representatives in every city and in the remote parts of the earth."—*Testimonies for the Church*, 6:24.

"In all countries and cities the gospel is to be proclaimed. . . .
"Churches are to be organized and plans laid for work to be done by the members of the newly organized churches."—*Evangelism* (Washington, D.C.: Review and Herald®, 1946), 19.

"Place after place is to be visited, church after church is to be raised up."—*Testimonies for the Church*, 7:20.

"The establishment of churches, the erection of meeting-houses and school-buildings, was extended from city to city, and the tithe was increasing to carry forward the work. Plants were made not only in one place, but in many places, and the Lord was working to increase His forces."—*Gospel Workers*, 435.

"Let not the work of establishing memorials for God in many places be made difficult and burdensome because the necessary means is withheld."—*Testimonies for the Church*, 9:132, 133.

"The people who bear His sign are to establish churches and institutions as memorials to Him."—*Testimonies for the Church*, 7:105.

"God's workers are to plant the standards of truth in every place to which they can gain access. . . . Memorials for Him are to be raised in America and in foreign countries."—*Selected Messages*, 1:112.

"Many of the members of our large churches are doing comparatively nothing. They might accomplish a good work if, instead of crowding together, they would scatter into places that have not yet been entered by the truth. Trees that are planted too thickly do not flourish. They are transplanted by the gardener, that they may have room to grow and not become dwarfed and sickly. The same rule would work well for our large churches. Many of the members are dying spiritually for want of this very work. They are becoming sickly and inefficient."—*Testimonies for the Church,* 8:244.

"This gospel missionary work is to keep reaching out and annexing new territory, enlarging the cultivated portions of the vineyard. The circle is to extend until it belts the world.

From town to town, from city to city, from country to country, the warning message is to be proclaimed, not with outward display, but in the power of the Spirit, by men of faith."—*Evangelism,* 19.

Chapter 14
From Obstacles to Opportunities[1]

"You will receive power when the Holy Spirit comes on you; and you will be my witnesses in Jerusalem, and in all Judea and Samaria, and to the ends of the earth."—Acts 1:8

"Place after place is to be visited, church after church is to be raised up."—Ellen G. White[2]

Church planting is a challenging enterprise. Claiming territory for Jesus most certainly solicits opposition from many sides. Realistic expectations are essential, and adequate support systems and coaching are very helpful. Our research revealed that those who commit themselves to church planting encounter significant obstacles, but as they depend on God, He answers with incredible blessings and rewards.[3] How will God overcome obstacles to bless your church and reach your city?

This chapter is based on data and interviews from the four conferences in North America that were most active in church planting during the past decade. It will address three common obstacles to church planting and show how God transforms them into amazing opportunities.[4]

Objection 1: We don't have enough people to plant a church

When the leaders of a local church consider planting another church, they often feel that they lack the necessary human resources. Jesus encouraged His followers that God provides as we commit to His mission: "The harvest is plentiful, but the workers are few. Ask the Lord of the harvest, therefore, to send out workers into his harvest field" (Luke 10:2).

The struggling Perry Seventh-day Adventist Church in Florida had dwindled to eight to ten elderly people. Then Patty Crouch was asked to serve as the lay pastor of that church. Driven by a burden to reach the young people in the community, Patty encouraged her church to step out in faith by selling their building and starting over on the other side of town.[5] They bought a trailer and began their "U-Turn" ministry to youth, with open mic programs, worship-and-game nights, and youth-led church services. Through the process of planting, God has given new life to this church and brought in more people than they thought was possible. The church now has eighty-some members, and it is one of the healthier congregations in the Florida conference, according to Allan Machado, former lay pastor coordinator and now Spanish coordinator of the Florida Conference.

Although smaller churches may feel they need to grow bigger before they give birth to another church, there are many cases that show that God blesses people's efforts to step out in faith. In 2007, the Houston Northwest church had about 125 people in attendance when they planted the Woodlands church. At the end of 2012, the mother church had an attendance of 196, and 71 were attending the daughter church.[6]

The small McKinney Spanish Seventh-day Adventist Church recognized that their city was experiencing explosive population growth,[7] yet that city had no English-speaking Adventist congregation. Just to the south, the Richardson Seventh-day Adventist Church had the personnel and the leadership they needed to start a church, but no place to worship. The two churches collaborated and in 2012 gave birth to a healthy new daughter church. The process excited and vitalized the parent churches.

Pastor Dan Serns said, "I'm praying that God impresses 5 percent of my members to become a part of the McKinney English Seventh-day Adventist Church." He said that while some might think that planting another Seventh-day Adventist church in the area might hurt nearby churches by competing with them for members, in fast-growing metro areas there are plenty people we need to reach for Jesus.

It is also apparent that God brings people to mother churches that step out in faith. The McKinney English Seventh-day Adventist church plant is the tenth that the Richardson Seventh-day Adventist Church has been involved with in the past fourteen years. When the Richardson church started planting new churches in January 2000, it had a weekly attendance of about 550 people. In 2012, after planting four churches and helping six others get started, its attendance had grown to 598.[8] At the end of 2012, the combined attendance of the Richardson church and all the churches it helped plant added up to more than seventeen hundred people.

In addition, between 2002 and 2010, 1,257 people were baptized,[9] and in July 2013, Richardson brought in its eight hundredth member. Its current membership is the highest it's been in the fifty-some years it has existed. Between 2000 and 2013, the North Dallas population grew by about 12.5 percent,[10] while Adventist church membership in that area grew by some 209 percent as a result of church multiplication. When this book was being written, the leaders of the Richardson Seventh-day Adventist Church were preparing to plant their fifth church.[11]

Often, churches that lose some of their members to a church planting grow back to their original size and more within six months to two years. The Mc-Donald Road Seventh-day Adventist Church, which is located in a rural area a few miles outside of Collegedale, Tennessee, had about eight hundred members. They wanted to grow, so they selected a community and began conducting Bible studies and doing other forms of evangelism there. Some four years later, they planted the East Ridge Seventh-day Adventist Church with a core group of about eighty people. Today the church plant is healthy and growing, and God has given the McDonald Road Seventh-day Adventist Church a free refill plus some extra. In fact, God has refilled the ranks of every church that has moved forward in faith and planted another church.

Objection 2: We don't have the money to plant a church

Most conferences don't have the funds to hire pastors whose sole responsibility is to plant new churches. Similarly, many churches are concerned about the financial resources they will lose when active members leave to start a new church. However, our research has revealed that church planting doesn't hurt the finances of either the conference or the mother church.

Conferences in which churches are planting other churches don't have to hire professional evangelists. When we studied the North American Division's four conferences most active in church planting, we found that all of them followed models in which lay members did the planting. Allan Machado said that Florida has eighty-seven lay pastors, many of whom have started new churches. Collectively they produced more than $3 million in tithe, while the total cost of the training, resources, and compensation for the travel expenditures of the lay leaders came to about $400,000 in 2012.[12] In other words, the Florida Conference's investment in church planting resulted in a net gain of more than two and a half million dollars.

Dr. Gerson Santos, executive secretary of the Greater New York Conference, says that when the conference was experiencing severe financial difficulties, they decided to increase their usage of the church-planting approach to doing evangelism, so they doubled the amount of money allocated to evangelism and special projects. Then Dr. Santos started a small group to train pastors and lay leaders to plant new churches.

In the eighteen months between the beginning of this program and my interview of Dr. Santos, these leaders planted seventeen churches of various types, including youth-led churches, ethnic churches, multiethnic churches, traditional churches, and urban mission centers.[13] At least one-third of these plants aimed at reaching secular postmodern professionals.

Santos said that the only expenses he incurred during the church-planting thrust were the meals that were provided for the leadership development small group and reimbursement for the travel expenses of lay planters. While the conference and its leaders and members were sacrificing financially, God blessed them by directing back to them enough money to pay off 70 percent of their debt during that time. The most exciting part for Santos was not the financial gain but the kingdom growth they experienced. "Baptisms are going through the roof," he said. "Last year was the best year in the New York mission ever!"[14]

Churches that plant other churches generate even more money to be used in God's mission. For example, in the Texas Conference, the tithe of the Richardson Seventh-day Adventist Church was $688,253 in 1999 ($948,492 in 2012 dollars). Fourteen years and ten church plants later, the combined tithe of all the eleven churches involved was about $2.24 million.[15] In all four conferences we studied, God provided significant financial dividends on their investment in church planting.

And it's not just the conferences that benefit by supporting church planting. The local churches that do the planting also benefit by it. Tom Evans, who oversaw the planting of more than one hundred churches in the Texas Conference, has confirmed this. He says, "Church planting doesn't have to cost the mother church anything. Some choose to assist in paying for the first evangelistic meeting or for a few months of rent to jumpstart the daughter church, but many successful church plants begin with nothing."[16]

In San Antonio, Texas, the Scenic Hills Seventh-day Adventist Church planted the Fil-Am International Seventh-day Adventist Church in 2003. Although the mother church didn't give any financial support to the plant, both mother and daughter churches have thrived. Sam Palomero, the lay leader of Fil-Am International, says they started with 25 people, and ten years later their membership was 226, and they averaged about 185 in attendance. "We are packed to the max now,"[17] Palomero says—and he goes on to state that in 2012 the church received $180,000 in tithe and $62,000 for the local church budget.

Like many churches, Scenic Hills was afraid of losing the financial support of key leaders who were going to plant the new church. They were in the middle of a building project, and some members felt they needed to keep all the personnel and resources they received to meet the needs of the Scenic Hills church. So the church decided to go ahead with the plant and trust God to provide the resources it would require. Rodney Mills, current pastor of the Scenic Hills church, noted the result. He said, "Planting didn't make a dent in the finances of the mother church. In fact, through planting we grew in both finances and members." Now, despite the launch of the new church, the attendance at the mother church amounts to about four hundred people. And the members of the Scenic Hills church are launching a Spanish church of about 120 people, and they have formed a Portuguese group as well.

Our study of the top four conferences in church planting revealed that in the period we studied, 2000 to 2012, some mother churches did have to make financial sacrifices because of planting a church. But none of them experienced financial difficulties so damaging as to affect the church's health permanently.

Objection 3: We're too busy to take on the planting of a church

Many churches pour lots of resources into a wide range of programs and activities. While every church does need a variety of constructive programs, it is important that we avoid losing sight of their purpose. In our research we discovered that church planting is the best "program" a church can do for evangelism, for discipleship and spiritual growth, and for reclaiming inactive members.

The possibility of increasing the harvest is the best reason to plant a new church, both for the mother church and for the daughter church. Extensive research in the Texas conference revealed that church plants had significantly better health than the established churches had. In fact, they were rated as being among the top 15 percent of all churches surveyed in the United States. In the Natural Church Development (NCD) survey, the category in which they were strongest was Needs Oriented Evangelism, and the questions in which they were strongest were "We encourage new Christians in our church to get involved in evangelism immediately" and "I try to deepen my relationships with people who do not yet know Jesus Christ."

The level of priority that the church plants gave to evangelism was also reflected in their budgets. Tom Evans noted, "Most church plants in Texas contribute at least 25 percent of their local church budget for evangelism. . . . Most established churches allocate less than five percent of their budget to evangelism."[18]

Although smaller and newer churches may not offer the level of programming that the larger, more established churches have, the smaller, newer churches actually have a higher growth potential. Jerry Fore, vice president of the Georgia-Cumberland Conference, did an extensive analysis of his conference that covered more than a decade. He says, "I discovered that the more established the church, the more members it takes to produce one baptism. On the other hand, the younger the church, the higher its potential for growth." This could be due to a number of factors, such as the necessity of reaping the harvest, the vitality that young churches tend to have, and their flexibility in methods and approaches.[19] Just like children, churches tend to hit their growth spurt while they are still young.[20]

Church planting develops leaders in both the planted church and in the mother church. Santos commented, "Our main goal is making disciples. As people grow, you need to put them in a place where they can use their passion and [the] new skills that they will develop. That would be a new church."

Santos told us about a church in New York City that had mostly elderly members. They decided they wanted to do something for young people, so they offered the use of their chapel in the church's basement. Within months, Fusion, a youth-led church, had been planted, and young disciples were stepping into leadership roles. "The head deacon is sixteen years old," Santos said, "and the head deaconess is thirteen."

The involvement of this church in street-corner ministry has resulted in many conversions and baptisms, even involving people who had been active in gangs. The church started with nineteen members and now has an attendance of sixty actively involved young people. "You remain in the church if you are involved," Santos says. "If you are not involved in ministry, you will come as a visitor." Within one year, Fusion planted the Zion youth-led church across town on Broadway in Manhattan.

Walton Zibanayi declares that his whole experience with God has grown in many ways through being involved as the leader of the McKinney English Seventh-day Adventist Church plant. One of the areas in which he grew was giving—providing money to the church. "When I was at Richardson, with its 750 members, it was easy to give the offering call and yet not be convicted personally to give much." Zibanayi returned tithe, but that was it. He felt that his finances didn't permit him to give any more for offerings.

However, with the new church, Walton says, "We realized that we had to personally give [so the church could pay its] bills. We started giving tithe plus an extra 10 percent for offerings. Three weeks later, I got a new job that gave an 80 percent increase in my salary." He says that he was hoping only for an extra 10 percent salary increase, but God gave him so much more. "Our family always struggled to pay all the expenses before. Now we don't even worry about it so much. God has taken care of us." Walton rejoiced over how God taught him to be faithful.

Churches across North America struggle with the reality that many of their members have become disenfranchised, disconnected, or inactive. Church plants give those individuals a mulligan—a chance to start over again.[21] Jerry Fore told us what he'd learned when he analyzed church plants in his conference: "It is harder for people to move into a mother church that is so well established in the status quo. New church plants have the opportunity to establish different structure and titles for programming."

People like new plants because they provide the opportunity to grow spiritually without any unfavorable memories or baggage and generally their members are open to new ideas. When the Collegedale Community Church was planted in an area surrounded by Adventist churches, some were afraid of losing members and tithe to the new plant. Collegedale Community Church specifically sought to reach the inactive Adventists who lived in the community. Now it has an attendance of more than twelve hundred. Eventually, all the churches in the area recovered and continued to grow. Fore noted, "Looking back, there have been no catastrophes in tithe or membership like some expected. In fact, there has been no decline in the Collegedale area at all."

God used church plants to reclaim inactive members in all the conferences we studied. Palomero, the lay pastor of the Fil-Am International Church in San Antonio, acknowledged that many of the members of his church were inactive before they came to the church plant and found it to be a place where they could connect with God.

In summary, we have looked at three significant objections to church planting: lack of people, lack of money, and schedules already full. We've seen that when churches are faithful to God, He transforms these obstacles into opportunities and blesses them with more than they ever had before.

Planting a church requires people to take a tremendous step of faith. But the rewards God provides far outweigh the risks. Through church planting, God adds people to His family, money for missions, effective evangelistic focus, spiritual growth, and reconnection to Him. Church planting is and has always been the most effective way to reach the harvest and move forward in mission. If we are faithful to God, He will be faithful in using us to accomplish miraculous things. What will God do through you and your church?

---

1. Dustin Serns, a Master of Divinity graduate from the Seventh-day Adventist Theological Seminary at Andrews University, aided in the writing of this chapter.

2. White, *Testimonies for the Church*, 7:20.

3. The challenge of reaching the rapidly growing population in North America is calling all levels of the church to wake up and begin a massive Seventh-day Adventist church-planting movement. Chapter 13 of this book, "Insights Gained From Planting Churches," compares the net growth of the Adventist churches with the growth of the United States population in the past century. To gain a realistic view, we studied the four conferences in the North American Division most involved in church planting during the last decade of the twentieth century—Texas, Georgia-Cumberland, Greater New York, and Florida. As we analyzed these conferences, we discovered powerful ways that God overcomes obstacles to move His work forward.

4. For additional reading about perceived obstacles to church planting, see Russell Burrill's "Myths of Church Planting," in *Rekindling a Lost Passion* (Fallbrook, Calif.: Hart Research Center, 1999), 98–101.

5. While relocating a church might be necessary sometimes, leaders should diligently and prayerfully seek to help church members make a difference wherever they are. This was Patty Crouch's ultimate intention.

6. *Texas Conference of Seventh-day Adventists Statistical Comparison by Pastoral District*, December 2012, 10.

7. McKinney's population grew 204 percent from 2000 to 2009 and was ranked as the second-fastest growing city in the United States. For the full article, see Dan Eakin, "Frisco, McKinney Top Two Fastest Growing Cities in America," *Star Local News*, February 14, 2012, http://www.pegasusnews.com/news/2012/feb/14/frisco-mckinney-top-fastest-growing-cities-america/?refscroll=1017.

8. *Texas Conference of Seventh-day Adventists Statistical Comparison by Pastoral District*, December 2012, 5.

9. It generally takes a new church plant a year or two to become established and bring results. The first church that Richardson planted was Metro North (since renamed Fairview Mosaic) in January 2000.

10. We limited our study of North Dallas, Texas, to include Richardson, Plano, McKinney, and Frisco because that is where the churches were planted. See http://www.city-data.com.

11. The Richardson Seventh-day Adventist Church is one example of a congregation that has followed the principle of church multiplication. Ed Stetzer and Warren Bird argue that churches should not only plant daughter churches but also aim to become "grandparent churches." See *Viral Churches: Helping Church Planters Become Movement Makers* (San Francisco: Jossey-Bass, 2010), 31–47. Ellen White affirms, "As churches are established, it should be set before them that it is even from among them that men must be taken to carry the truth to others and raise new churches." *Testimonies for the Church*, 3:205.

12. Allan Machado, personal interview, September 10, 2013.

13. This strategy is in harmony with Stuart Murray's argument that multiple kinds of churches are needed to reach different kinds of people, especially in a postmodern age. See *Church Planting: Laying Foundations* (Scottsdale, Ariz.: Harold Press, 2001), 156–180.

14. Dr. Gerson Santos, telephone interview, October 4, 2013.

15. *Texas Conference of Seventh-day Adventists Statistical Comparison by Pastoral District,* December 2012, 5, 6.

16. Tom Evans, personal interview, October 21, 2013. This observation confirmed the continued validity of Dudley and Gruesbeck's findings in 1989. In a comprehensive study of Seventh-day Adventist church plants in the 1970s and 1980s, they discovered that receiving financial aid from another church did not make much of a difference in the growth and success of the church plant. They noted: "The differences given are too small to be significant," and "only a minority of churches surveyed received such aid." Roger L. Dudley and Clarence B. Gruesbeck, *Plant a Church, Reap a Harvest* (Boise, Idaho: Pacific Press®, 1989), 39. Lyle Schaller argues, "The less we make our church plantings dependent on subsidy, the more dependable they'll be. . . . Direct or indirect financial aid can be addictive to both the givers and receivers." *44 Questions for Church Planters,* 141.

17. Sam Palomero, telephone interview, October 4, 2013.

18. Tom Evans, *Implementation of a Conference-wide Church Planting Strategy With the Texas Conference* (DMin. diss., Seventh-day Adventist Theological Seminary, 2013), 115, 116.

19. Dudley and Gruesbeck also discovered that newer churches had flexibility and vitality and were able to reap the harvest effectively. *Plant a Church, Reap a Harvest,* 17–27. Russell Burrill writes about the life cycle of a church, which means that as the church grows older, it will ultimately need revival. See *Waking the Dead* (Silver Spring, Md.: Review and Herald®, 2004), 31–35.

20. Aubrey Malphurs also outlines this phenomenon in his description of the life cycle of the church. See *Planting Growing Churches for the 21st Century* (Grand Rapids, Mich.: Baker, 2004), 32–34.

21. Our research affirmed this well-established church-planting concept. Dudley and Gruesbeck observed, "Numerous studies have shown that 60 to 80 percent of new adult members of new congregations are persons who were not actively involved in the life of any worshiping congregation immediately prior to joining that new mission. . . . Some of these new adult members are youth who once dropped out of the church in their teens or early twenties. Later, as parents, they want their children to have some religious training. Preferring not to attend their parents' church, these young adults look for new types of worship and new experiences of renewal. Other former attenders do not want to come back to the church where they are embarrassed to return or fear that other members will not accept them. On the other hand, such people find acceptance in a new congregation where believers are used to welcoming new members." Dudley and Gruesbeck, *Plant a Church, Reap a Harvest,* 20. See also Schaller, *44 Questions for Church Planters,* 27, 28.

Ten Simple Steps Toward Getting Started

1. Develop love for the lost. They matter to God and must matter to us.
2. Cultivate a church-planting philosophy. Study the subject in the Bible, in the writings of Ellen White, and in some practical books in order to develop your church's position on church planting.
3. Keep praying that God will enlarge your territory by expanding your influence and evangelistic outreach through church planting.
4. Through sermons, board meetings, newsletters, and so forth, educate the leaders and lay members of your church about the value, needs, and benefits of starting a new church. Commit as a church to work toward planting.
5. Claim the promise in Matthew 9:37, 38 that God will send out workers into the harvest field by bringing you leaders who will take on this project. Invest deeply in their spiritual growth and their development as leaders.
6. Identify, elect, and mentor the church-plant leader and core group. The core group can begin planning, doing evangelism, and recruiting members while continuing involvement in their home church or churches.
7. Get the training you need. For training events and resources, go to the North American Division Evangelism Institute Web site at http://www.nadei.org.
8. Study the demographic needs and trends of your area to determine the best location for planting a new church. One of the best ways to reach the people in any community is to plant a church there. Work to connect any Adventists in that area with the new plant.
9. Set aside some resources to help the young church secure a building to buy or rent and/or to purchase evangelistic supplies and equipment.
10. Develop the strategy that best fits your church. Set it in motion and move forward in faith. Pray consistently for the harvest and for God's leading and blessing.

Conclusion
Your Best Days Are Ahead

"Be strong and courageous. Do not be afraid; do not be discouraged, for the LORD *your God will be with you wherever you go."—Joshua 1:9*

" 'I know the plans I have for you,' declares the LORD, *'plans to prosper you and not to harm you; plans to give you hope and a future.' "—Jeremiah 29:11*

This book has presented ways in which churches can fulfill the purpose for which Christ created them through leadership, relationships, evangelism, worship, preaching, and church planting. What follows is a reflection on each of these gifts and how they work together when we allow our hearts to be infected with God's love for people and choose to be a part of His great mission.

Effective and efficient leadership

The leaders in the church set the tone it presents by instilling the vision and helping to train members to live out the Great Commission of Matthew 28:19, 20 in all areas of their lives.

Focus on instilling the vision of ministry and evangelism. Every year in my seminary classes I ask the students whether they've heard a series of sermons on the mission of the church. Unfortunately, the answer is almost always No. As spiritual leaders, our administrators and pastors are in the best position to instill the realization that lost people matter to God and they should matter to us. The mission of the church ought to be front and center—and cast in creative and compelling ways. As the leaders cast this vision of reaching lost souls, it must be accompanied by an emphasis on the urgency of our time. The early church was caught up with the conviction that Jesus was coming soon, and that conviction drove them to take His message to the entire world. They did it with passion, conviction, and urgency. People who love Jesus and have a clear vision of their destiny will do anything for His cause.

Train, equip, and motivate the laity for ministry and evangelism. The main role of church leaders is to train and equip the laity for evangelism. I have been asking my students whether there is a systematic program of training and equipping in their local churches. Out of the hundreds of people I've asked in the past fourteen years, fewer than ten have said their local church has any kind of training program for ministry and evangelism.

Paul defines the roles of pastor and teacher as equippers of the saints for the work of service, to the building up of the body of Christ.[1] Jesus spent three and half years training people for ministry. Ellen White wrote: "Every church should be a training school for Christian workers. . . . There should not only be teaching, but actual work under experienced instructors. Let the teachers lead the way in working among the people, and others, uniting with them, will learn from their example. One example is worth more than many precepts."[2]

She also emphasizes that "ministers should not do the work which belongs to the church, thus wearying themselves, and preventing others from performing their duty. They should teach the members how to labor in the church and in the community."[3]

Churches grow when laypeople are passionate about the mission of Jesus Christ and are active in sharing His love. Lack of member involvement in evangelism can be attributed to weak spirituality, lack of vision, fear of rejection, busyness, disdain of traditional methods of evangelism such as door-to-door visitation and public meetings, a professionalizing of evangelism, and doubt that people are interested in the gospel and particularly in our unique message. Some people may even be embarrassed by their local church. Many of these barriers to member involvement can be counteracted through training for the purpose of equipping and motivating the congregation.

Growing the family: relationships, church growth, and evangelism

Many people, especially the young, are spiritual and are looking for an experience with God, but they are not inclined to look for it in the church.[4] Because people don't feel comfortable coming into our churches, we must be willing to go out and meet them where they are. It is by seeing how we experience God in our everyday lives that they will begin to see how they, too, can come to know and love God. This is shown by making evangelism a way of life and using a variety of methods to reach people.

Make evangelism a way of life. When I ask people in my training seminars the question "When was the last time your church did evangelism?" the answer I get most often is "We had evangelistic meetings last year" (or "three years ago," or "ten years ago"). Most think of evangelism as an event. In reality, however, evangelism is a way of life. It takes place anytime, anywhere, by anyone, and under any circumstances.

When in my seminar I have the students read the book of Acts and list all the times the author says the believers evangelized or ministered, they often come up with more than fifty or sixty different experiences and methods of evangelism and ministry. The ultimate core value for the early Christians was Jesus. That's why they lived and breathed evangelism and ministry. The goal of the early church was to show the world how to experience Jesus. They believed that nothing on earth or in heaven would stop them. Jesus was everything to them.

Use a variety of methods and strategies to reach people. For many years our church has relied heavily on public evangelism as the way to grow our churches and to fulfill the Great Commission. Many of the pastors, leaders, researchers, and lay members I interviewed believe that our strategies and techniques of public evangelism worked very well in the past but work less well today. Monte Sahlin, a well-known researcher in the field of Adventist culture and trends, has come to the same conclusion. He says that if the church focuses solely on traditional public evangelism to evangelize the world, we risk ignoring and ostracizing the vast majority of people.[5]

Today we have an entirely new generation whose views differ radically from those of the past. We aren't keeping up with the unique opportunities of today. This new era is challenging us to color outside the lines of the old evangelism—to try something more effective. While we must keep the traditional methods in our toolbox, we must also use *every* avenue to win people for Jesus Christ. Public evangelism, strongly connected with friendship evangelism and saturated with prayer and the Holy Spirit, has a definite place in our outreach efforts. The more tools the church utilizes, the more effective it will be.

We see that the early church grew by employing every means available to them to evangelize the world; we would do well to follow their example and experience. The church today does need to use a variety of methods to win people.[6] It must be open to friendship evangelism;[7] meaningful Sabbath schools, worship services, and public evangelistic meetings; and building authentic spiritual disciples.[8]

Having a variety of programs serves at least two purposes. First, it creates avenues through which believers can share their faith in a natural way. Second, multiple kinds of evangelism reach various kinds of people, at least some of which might not have been the right one to reach everyone. Every event, every ministry, every activity should be done with the purpose of connecting people with God.

Awe-inspiring worship

Church renewal is always connected with worship renewal.[9] In *Opening the Front Door: Worship and Church Growth,* James Emery White makes the observation that church growth and renewal are usually connected with worship experiences.[10] It seems evident that most people are hungry for dynamic, inspiring worship. Many are longing to have an encounter with God, to feel His presence and live His power.

George Barna makes it clear that the number one expectation that people have regarding the church is to feel the presence of God.[11] Our churches are urged to pay much more attention to their worship services and to continually bathe their members and guests with prayer so they can encounter the presence of God. Thom S. Rainer shows that the worship service contributes in a very positive way toward evangelism, discipleship, and assimilation.[12] Every time the church is intentional about worship renewal, it becomes healthy and starts to grow.

Transformational and engaging preaching

Worship is essential to the health of the church and its members, yet it can't take the place of the preaching of God's Word. The church today still needs preaching to be a priority. Paul told the Romans, "Faith comes from hearing the message, and the message is heard through the word about Christ" (Romans 10:17). God has chosen to make Himself known to us through preaching. The apostle Paul was emphatic about it. He told Timothy to "preach the word!" (2 Timothy 4:2, NKJV).

When Paul was witnessing on Mars Hill in Athens, Greece, he could have used drama to make his points. After all, drama was an invention of the Greeks. Paul could have had someone present "The Gospel in Three Acts," or he could have had it put to music. But he didn't do either of those things. Instead, he preached. Music, singing, and the arts all have their place, but they are nowhere near as important as the preaching and teaching of the Word of God. I know this to be true, not only because the Bible says it is, but also from personal experience.

I've had the privilege of teaching and preaching for more than thirty-five years from China to London and from Michigan to Sydney; and in all kinds of venues, from large arenas to Bible studies in a home with a young family as my only audience. From what I've seen in all these places, I can tell you that it is by hearing God's Word preached that lives are touched.

The first time I had the privilege of preaching the gospel, I saw the power of God at work. My life was touched by the teaching and preaching of God's Word. Years later, I still am touched when I hear messages from the Word of God. I love to listen to preaching; I listen to sermons and messages from different pastors all the time.

Preaching is used to help the listeners grow in their walk with God. One way to make sure that your preaching is continually focused on the spiritual nurturing and maturing of your congregation is by using the sermonic-year planning method. This requires you to look below the surface of your community and find areas that should be addressed. Remember the words written to the Hebrews, "Let us move beyond the elementary teachings about Christ and be taken forward to maturity, not laying again the foundation of repentance from acts that lead to death, and of faith in God" (Hebrews 6:1).

Being in two places at once: church planting

All experts agree that church planting is the most effective means of church growth. According to C. Peter Wagner, "The single most effective evangelistic methodology under heaven is planting new churches."[13] In *44 Questions for Church Planters,* Lyle Schaller writes, "Without exception, the growing denominations have been those that stress church planting." He goes on to write that "church planting continues to be the most useful and productive component of any denominational church-growth strategy."[14]

David Olson says he has discovered that *up to their fortieth year,* new churches tend to grow, attracting young people, providing synergy, and helping to raise a new generation of lay leaders, among many other things.[15]

Olson also stresses that church planting is needed because established churches most likely will continue to plateau or decline.[16] Therefore, church planting should be put in the DNA of every local church and conference. Ellen White laid it out clearly. She wrote that God has placed the burden of raising churches "upon all who believe."[17] Every congregation, large or small, has the calling and the ability to plant churches.

Intimate and passionate spirituality

Although I haven't given the topic of spirituality its own section in this book, a renewed heart and intentional prayer are essential elements of every chapter. Consequently, we must prioritize spirituality and renewal. An emphasis on spirituality and revival should be the main work of the church. Ellen White strongly connected renewal with an ongoing experience with Jesus. "A revival of true godliness among us is the greatest and most urgent of all our needs. To seek this should be our first work. . . . It is our work, by confession, humiliation, repentance, and earnest prayer, to fulfill the conditions upon which God has promised to grant us His blessing."[18]

The church must increase its investment in the spiritual development of our pastors, leaders, and members. The emphasis of the church should not be on building programs but on growing fully devoted disciples of Jesus—people who have a passion for Him. The most important asset the church has is its members. When those members are spiritually healthy, growing, trained, and equipped, they will do great things for God. The book of Acts tells us that because of the love of the New Testament church for Jesus and the urgency of the message, they gave of their time, talents, possessions, and even their lives for the cause of

God.[19] Today, people are looking to the church to give them what will satisfy their spiritual needs. If their needs aren't met there, they will go elsewhere in search of spiritual satisfaction.

Intentional prayer life

Church growth is always closely related to prayer and the power of the Holy Spirit. Ellen White clearly related renewal to prayer. "A revival need be expected only in answer to prayer. While the people are so destitute of God's Holy Spirit, they cannot appreciate the preaching of the Word; but when the Spirit's power touches their hearts, then the discourses given will not be without effect."[20]

God specializes in doing the impossible. The early church didn't grow because of programs or talents or resources; they grew because of prayer and the Holy Spirit.[21] Let us remember "the word of the LORD to Zerubbabel: 'Not by might nor by power, but by my Spirit,' says the LORD Almighty" (Zechariah 4:6).

Thom Rainer, in *High Expectations,* shows that praying churches tend to grow and to retain a higher percentage of their members.[22] In an upbeat note, Ellen White wrote: "Prayer and faith will do what no power upon earth can accomplish. We need not be so anxious and troubled. The human agent cannot go everywhere, and do everything that needs to be done. . . . Earnest prayer and faith will do for us what our own devising cannot do."[23]

Your church has a fantastic future

Your church may be facing serious challenges that will require a re-evaluation of your values and methods. As we consider a way to move forward in the future, it is crucial for us to understand that there's only one Person who can overcome our weaknesses and challenges—the Lord Jesus Christ. "Workers for Christ are never to think, much less to speak, of failure in their work. The Lord Jesus is our efficiency in all things; His Spirit is to be our inspiration; and as we place ourselves in His hands, to be channels of light, our means of doing good will never be exhausted. We may draw upon His fullness, and receive of that grace which has no limit."[24]

So, as we go into the future, let us go with Him.

---

1. Ephesians 4:12. See also 2 Timothy 2:2, "The things which you have heard from me in the presence of many witnesses, entrust these to faithful men who will be able to teach others also" (NASB).

2. White, *The Ministry of Healing,* 149.

3. Ellen G. White, *Historical Sketches of the Foreign Missions of the Seventh-day Adventists* (Basle: Imprimerie Polyglotte, 1886), 291.

4. Reggie McNeal, *The Present Future* (San Francisco: Jossey-Bass, 2003), 4, 5. See also James H. Rutz, *The Open Church* (Auburn, Maine: The SeedSowers, 1992), 3.

5. Monte Sahlin, interview by S. Joseph Kidder, Berrien Springs, Michigan, September 24, 2014.

6. Two of several authors who note the need for various evangelism methods are Lyle E. Schaller, *44 Ways to Increase Church Attendance,* 49–63, and Thom S. Rainer, *The Book of Church Growth: History, Theology, and Principles* (Nashville, Tenn.: Broadman Press, 1993), 239–247.

7. Kidder, "The Power of Relationships in Evangelism." See also Win Arn, *The Master's Plan for Making Disciples* (Pasadena, Calif.: Church Growth Press, 1982), 33–54.

8. Bill Hull, *The Disciple-Making Church* (Old Tappan, N.J.: F. H. Revell, 1988), 19–27.

9. Walter C. Kiser Jr., *Quest for Renewal: Personal Revival in the Old Testament* (Chicago: Moody Press, 1986), 11–25.

10. James Emery White, *Opening the Front Door: Worship and Church Growth* (Nashville, Tenn.: Convention, 1992), 62–64.

11. George Barna, "How to Reach Post-Moderns," Adventist Ministerial Convention, Myrtle Beach, N.C., January 20, 2009.

12. Rainer, *The Book of Church Growth,* 20.

13. C. Peter Wagner, *Church Planting for a Greater Harvest* (Ventura, Calif.: Regal, 1990), 11.

14. Schaller, *44 Questions,* 20.

15. David T. Olson, *The American Church in Crisis* (Grand Rapids, Mich.: Zondervan, 2008), 155, 156.

16. Ibid., 142–157.

17. White, *Medical Ministry,* 315.

18. White, *Selected Messages,* 1:121.

19. Roberta Hestenes, *The Power to Make Things New* (Waco, Tex.: Word Books, 1986), 79–90.

20. White, *Selected Messages,* 1:121.

21. Randy Maxwell, *If My People Pray* (Boise, Idaho: Pacific Press®, 1995), 31.

22. Thom S. Rainer, *High Expectations: The Remarkable Secret for Keeping People in Your Church* (Nashville, Tenn.: Broadman and Hollman, 1999), 174, 175.

23. Ellen G. White, *Manuscript Releases* (Washington, D.C.: E. G. White Estate, 1990), 8:218.

24. White, *Gospel Workers,* 19.